BEHIND *the* COVERING

A World of Difference

By Sharon Spring

An Inspiring Story on Faith, Love,
Hope and Redemption

xulon PRESS

Introduction to the Mennonite Beliefs

Who Are the Mennonites?

The Mennonite Church is a Christian faith. The membership of the Mennonite Church is scattered over sixty countries with an estimated membership of more than a million. Twenty formally organized Mennonite groups are in America, all of which have their origins in the Anabaptist (a member of any various Protestant sects) movement. Mennonites retained much of their Anabaptist philosophy (opposes infant baptism but requires adult baptism). There are about 100,000 members and over 1,000 places of worship in the Eastern United States. Pennsylvania contains more than forty percent of all the members in the United States.

Among the many branches of Mennonites, there is a wide variety of tradition and practice today. Some dress in "plain" clothes, but the others embellish the traditional styles or disregard them altogether. The Amish are an offshoot of the Mennonites. The Amish broke away from the Mennonites in 1693 because the Mennonites were becoming too liberal. The Amish ban automobiles, radios, TV, electricity, and fancy clothing. Their tradition demands bonnets, braids, and beards.

The keynote of worship is simplicity. Sunday school and preaching services are held in meeting houses, which usually are of simple architecture. A center aisle in some churches divide men from the women. There is excellent singing by the whole congregation under the guidance of a song leader.

The Mennonites believe that Jesus Christ is the eternal Son of God and that He was conceived of the Holy Spirit and born to a virgin—the perfect God man. He was without sin, the divinely appointed substitute and representative of sinful man. He paid the penalty for man's sins by His death on the cross, making the only adequate atonement for sin by the shedding of His blood, and thus reconciling man in God. They also believe that Christ was raised from the dead, ascended to glory, and "ever liveth to make intercession for us." The Mennonites believe that man is saved alone by grace through faith in the finished work of Christ; that he is justified from all things on the ground of His shed blood; and that through the new birth he becomes a child of God, partaker of eternal life and blessed with all spiritual blessings in Christ. They believe in the Deity and personality of the Holy Spirit (referring to Jesus): He convinces the world of sin, righteousness, and of judgment; He indwells and comforts the believer, guides them into all truth, empowers him for service, and enables him to live a life of righteousness.

The Mennonite church baptizes by pouring water, but that alone is not considered an assurance of entrance to Heaven. It is rather a symbol of what has taken place on the inside of the person being baptized—repentance, forsaking of sin, the world, and the devil, with an eternal pledge of obedience to Christ and the church. For this reason, infant baptism has no place among the Mennonites.

The Mennonites observe the Lord's Supper twice annually as a memorial of our Lord's suffering and death. Unlike members of most churches, Mennonites wash one another's feet and observe the holy kiss. This usually occurs in connection with the communion service. These practices are based on Scripture John 13:1-10 and 1 Peter 5:14.

The Mennonite faith places strong moral obligations on its members.

Rules and Disciplines

For the brethren—they believe the plain coats, hats, and dark footwear best express the principle of nonconformity for all brethren and also give witness to the simple life. Fleeting fads, sportswear, improper bodily exposure, and modern styles in hair-cuts are to be avoided. Many Mennonite men, though, follow conventional hairstyles and wear ready-made clothes. Some ministers and members wear the "plain coat," which buttons straight to the top and has no lay-down collar. Their conscience tells them the tie is worldly.

The conservative Mennonites believe the plain cape dress and dark footwear is the best expression of modesty and nonconformity for all sisters. The cape dress consists of an extra piece of cloth over the shoulders, fastened at the waistline and shoulders. The bonnet should be plain and suitable to be worn as a protective covering in public. The hair arrangement should exemplify humility and meekness and be free from modern styles and fads. The Mennonite dress is not nearly as distinctive as that of the Amish.

Women in more traditional groups wear white caps and prayer veiling, a practice based on a passage from the Bible. "Any woman who prays or prophesies with her head unveiled dishonors her head" (1 Cor. 11:5). Head coverings symbolize for them the functional relationship of God's order in creation—God, Christ, man, woman. These "coverings" are worn always throughout the day. The most distinguishing feature of the woman is the general absence of makeup and jewelry.

Mennonite women have serenity in their faces. They have kindness, peace, and assurance in their lives that most people desire. Their social life is a satisfying blend of work and church life. Not being afraid of hard labor, they eat well and provide amply for their households. Sisters shall not cut their hair, wear slacks, shorts, or fashionable headdresses, short sleeves or low necklines. Dresses not reaching well below the knees or clothes that expose the form of the body are all considered immodest. Members shall respond to admonition and scriptural teaching of the ministry or be disciplined

(Heb. 13:17). They are well known for their orderly, neat, clean and spotless houses, both inside and out.

Disasters by fire, tornado, death, heavy financial loss, and other emergencies are alleviated by a system of mutual aid and by generous labor and gifts. A Mennonite statement to the Pennsylvania Assembly in 1775 said, "It is our principle to feed the hungry and give the thirsty drink. We have dedicated ourselves to serve all men in everything that can be helpful to the preservation of men's lives, but we find no freedom in giving or assisting in anything by which men's lives are destroyed or hurt."

Mennonites are well known for their stand in peace. Many choose not to participate in military spending, and a few withhold a percentage of their annual income taxes that would go for military spending. Serving in military service and training, either in combatant or noncombatant service, conflicts with the biblical doctrine of nonresistance. Members who go into military training or service forfeit their membership.

Education

Most of the Mennonite churches today strongly support education. The Mennonites have three colleges and also operate twelve church high schools and approximately seventy elementary schools. There are a few Mennonite conferences that believe in education to the ninth grade only, same as Amish.

Occupations and Contributions

Less than half of all Mennonites are farmers. They own and use the latest machinery like other enterprising farmers. The automobile, the tractor, the airplane, and almost any machine or device may be used, so long as it saves time or contributes to the welfare of the family. Work, thrift, and family go together as their saying is "Work makes life sweet."

Driven to the hills and poorer lands of Europe by their persecutors, earlier Mennonites were forced to learn intensive farming methods for survival. In almost all countries where they have lived, they have become noted as skillful farmers. Mennonites who came to this country contributed their agricultural techniques to America. Lancaster County, Pennsylvania, became the "garden spot of the world" mainly because of the Mennonites contributions. Not all members are farmers. There are also doctors, bankers, contractors, business men, artists, composers, writers, editors, social workers, engineers, electricians, researchers, public accountants, and interior designers.

The Mennonites were among the first in America to sign a petition against slavery. They believe that in a world of violence, racism, and extreme selfishness, God calls them to love and be helpful to all men. As followers of Christ, they can have no part in race discrimination in any form.

The first paper mill in America was built by a Mennonite minister, William Rittenhouse. The largest book published in colonial America was the Mennonite martyr book, *Martyrs Mirror* (Ephrata, 1747).

The most notable economic contribution of the Mennonites to the New World was intensive agriculture combined with family-centered farms. They abhorred plantation agriculture and slaveholding. Mennonite pioneers introduced the use of compost, simple forms of crop rotation, and legume crops as a method of restoring soil fertility. By combining an agrarian economy and the worship of God, Mennonites built communities of togetherness. Learning to live cooperatively under the influence of home and church has always been important to them.

Restrictions

As "plain people" they live austerely and without many pleasures. Members shall not indulge in the world's methods of pleasure seeking, amusements, and entertainments, patronizing or taking part in fairs, parades, circuses, commercial moving pictures, theaters, mixed public bathing, regularly organized contesting ball teams, dancing, card parties, gambling, and such.

Membership in secret societies and lodges is not permitted. Membership in labor unions, because of the coercive practices, is to be avoided. Forms of life insurance which make merchandise of life for material gain are forbidden. In many ways such participation transgresses the teaching of the Scriptures as related to separation. The brotherhood is urged to maintain faith in God and His provisions through the church in this materialistic age and avoid the unscriptural entanglements with world organizations.

The Mennonite Conference cautions the brotherhood to discriminate in the general use of the radio so that the spiritual life and testimony of the Christian home and church will be safeguarded. Many of the programs produced for the radio audiences are not intended for the spiritual uplifting of the Christian home and church.

Television is a modern means of communication with great potential in molding the thinking and the character of both young and old. While television is used sometimes to promote worthy causes, by far the greater part of what it brings into the home is entertainment, propaganda and commercials. Television programs are often destructive to the spiritual life and undermine the principles of separation from the world, the precepts of Christian morality, the proper respect for human life, and the sanctity of marriage and the Christian home. The Mennonites believe that the evil influence of television greatly outweighs that which is good. For the spiritual protection, blessing, and testimony of the church, the Mennonite Conference asks the brotherhood to abstain from the use and ownership of television.

The Mennonites believe the production and use of tobacco seriously affects our Christian witness and has harmful effects on the body. Members are asked to abstain from the use, distribution and production of tobacco.

The church wants their members to avoid jury duty as much as possible. In cases where capital punishment is involved, it is forbidden.

If a Mennonite member marries one who is divorced, she or he forfeits their membership. Anyone married to and living with a divorced spouse, cannot be received into the church fellowship.

DEDICATION

This book is dedicated to

My Heavenly Father

Thank You for being so patient and so, so forgiving. It is Your unfailing faithfulness that has carried me through all the obstacles life has tossed my way. When the church rejected me and then my fear of being rejected by humanity became part of my life, I did not really feel accepted by the world. I was continually mistreated by people, but it was Your persistent love for me that brought me back into your arms. I finally have love, peace, and joy in my heart again. You are the saving grace to having a fulfilled life!

My Earthly Father and Mother (both deceased)

Reflecting back on my childhood and teenage days, I will always remember my parents as the best, wonderful people. They served the community well and really cared about people while on their mission journey. My parents were my rock, so strong and loving. I attribute all my success in life to their moral teachings. About good and evil and standing up for doing right did not come to me through lectures and sermons, although I heard plenty of them at church and revival meetings. They came through my parents' attempt to establish and strengthen their relationship with the Lord. I thank the Lord for blessing me with wonderful parents. They gave me my God-fearing foundation to start life with, and with this solid foundation of faith and love I have survived the ups and downs of life. Our prayers before all meals and our wonderful conversations around the dinner table and evening devotions gave me courage to maintain my Christian walk as a young child into adolescence. Thank you, thank you, Mom and Dad, for your personal inspiration and your straight and narrow walk with the Lord. Mom and Dad, you are truly examples of what godly parents should be like. Thank you for all your prayers. Finally your waiting is over—I am back in the arms of the Lord.

My Three Children

God has blessed me with wonderful children. My children were my inspiration to keep going during most of the years of living my life without God, although I did feel his presence here and there as He touched my life through the love of His people around me. I am greatly sorry for all the hurt I have caused my family, especially my children, whose home was *broken* also, due to not keeping God in my life. For my children and to all who read my story, never give up hope, for God is in the business of restoring broken lives.

My Nieces and Nephew (Richard's children)

Due to our broken family, some of my nieces and a nephew did not have the opportunity to really get to know their grandparents. Hopefully, after reading my story, they will finally know what wonderful and kind people they were.

Jeanette Goodman

Jeanette, the finest godly woman without a doubt, has been a blessing to me and my sister Ann Marie. She was my comforter on that horrible Sunday morning. After the congregation received communion which I was denied, and I sat down on the pew and sobbed, she led me to my knees in prayer as we washed each other's feet. I have always remembered her kind words, saying, "God loves you and always will" as we exchanged the "Holy Kiss." Today she is still a very good friend to Ann Marie and me. Jeanette really cares. She listens, prays for our healing, and she loves us unconditionally like our God! Actually, Jeanette is the only Mennonite friend that Ann Marie and I have. Isn't God awesome that He kept Jeanette in my sister's life? God has remained in my sister's life and kept her from becoming discouraged about life through having Jeanette's friendship. I am sure Jeanette is one of God's chosen women who will see the pearly gates! Jeanette, you are a godsend, our angel! You have been Ann Marie's comforter since our mom passed away! Thank you for being an awesome friend. We love you. You have left a positive mark on Ann Marie and me.

To Everyone Else who knew my lifelong struggles and were there for me.

Bibliography

John A. Hostelter (1974) Mennonite Life (Herald Press, Scottdale PA)

Martha B Shank (2012) Bible Truths with Aunt Martha Jane

(TGS International), Berlin, OH

Mennonite Church/Statement of Christian Doctrine and Rules and Discipline of the Lancaster Conference/Adopted by the Lancaster Conference of the Mennonite Church at Special Session at the Mellinger Mennonite Church on July 17, 1968

All Scripture quotations are taken from the King James Version or the NIV Study Bible

NOTE FROM THE AUTHOR

*W*riting my personal story about my Mennonite upbringing and my life experiences involves very tough choices. My family and my personal relationships defined my life. Some were good, and some were bad. I struggled with what to write about and what not to write about, so I have decided to tell it all. I have made many wrong turns throughout my journey living without God.

The multiple paths I traveled after leaving the Mennonite faith has not been the straight and narrow. As I thought about writing my story, people and places and events flooded my memory. I was not sure that I wanted to write this book at all, but if sharing my experiences can bless one soul and give one person the vision of repentance and forgiveness, it is worth the risk of telling my deepest secrets.

As a very young child, I knew I had love and compassion for all humanity; we were all equal in God's eyes. I was a very happy child and always wanted to please my family and the church. My parents were very dedicated to God, the church, and of course our family. I was surrounded by love, kindness, and compassion. I wanted to share to the world the joy of having God in your life and Jesus in your heart brings immeasurable peace and happiness.

Being denied communion when I was seventeen years old turned my world upside down. I not only lost my love for God and the church, but I would also lose my trust in Jesus, who I thought would be my friend forever. I now trusted no one! Some may point fingers and say the church mishandled this, but let God do the judging. For over thirty years I lived my life without God, and my parents were not involved really in my life because they did not approve of my worldly lifestyle.

I've passed through many big storms in my life; some people may not believe all my stormy years, but I feel very blessed to have survived them all to share my story. I am sure my mother's prayers kept me safe and covered from all the horrible consequences that could have happened to me due to not having God in my life. Looking back, God's grace and mercy have done more for me than my mind can comprehend. Most of my horrific storms were due to the effects of what alcohol abuse can do to a person, a relationship, and a family. As I share my testimony with you, I pray that you read with an open mind and not with judgment and empathy not sympathy. I am hoping that my story will give hope to others who might be dealing with some of the same struggles I have overcome. I am sure my mother's and father's prayers and my Heavenly Father's persistent love for me put me back on the right road so I may enjoy the "good life."

God's greatest desire is the redemption of the souls of men. Desiring only to enhance His great purpose, I present to you *Behind the Covering—A World of Difference.*

ACKNOWLEDGMENTS

*A*s I reflect back on my life since early childhood years to the present, there are family and friends who have made a strong impact on me telling my story. My friends wanted to know more about the Mennonite faith and why I was banned from youth groups and was denied communion. Many of my family members encouraged me to tell my story since they were so young and never knew my struggles I lived with everyday.

They are:

My younger siblings They never really knew why I left the Mennonite church since they were much younger than I. They did see though the depth of sorrow our family portrayed for many, many years. Our family was broken. I am ready to share my pain-filled journey toward victory with them.

Donna (a friend since grade school). I have known Donna since third grade. She lived with Mennonites (in foster care) for eight years due to losing her father from a heart attack and her mother was involved in a serious car accident. She is still a good friend today and has been cheering me on to finish my story.

Patty (a friend since middle school). Patty is the friend who shot an arrow at me in the eighth grade. Who would have known a wayward arrow would lead me to a best friend forever. Patty also has been encouraging me to write my story and is my biggest cheerleader!

Ally (a friend in middle school and high school). I will never forget Ally's expression when I turned around to say something to George, who had thrown a spitball at my covering in seventh grade. She looked so sad for me. I saw tears filling her eyes. Her facial expression has never left me in all of these years. Ally and I reconnected several years ago. I am very blessed to have her in my life. I know God had His hand in our reconnecting. Ally also concurs that I should share my story.

Barbie (a friend). Barbie has been encouraging me to finish my book since she thinks I can help others who have been wounded and left by the wayside to fend for themselves. I have known Barbie for twenty years. She also had a Decorating Den Franchise, and we were always there for each other.

My eldest son He thought I had a great inspirational story to share, since I was raised in a very sheltered environment (Mennonite) that didn't believe in women working outside the home and where even owning a TV set was taboo.

My youngest son He encouraged me to finish my story since the Amish and Mennonite faith is being flaunted on television. He thinks I should share my story giving people a better insight of who the Mennonites are and what they believe.

Jennifer (a niece). She was always curious about the family history. She never really knew her extended family except for me and my children. She felt like an outsider; she didn't think her grandparents really even cared about her.

A complete stranger This person approached me in the recovery waiting room at Washington Hospital Center (when I was waiting to see my father after his open heart surgery, along with all my Mennonite siblings and their spouses), and asked me, "How are you involved with the Mennonites?" I informed her they were my siblings. She asked me for my phone number and said she has so many questions about the Mennonites and what they believe. She called and I answered all her questions. Her last words to me, "You need to write your story and tell it all."

My Heavenly Father—His Word (the Bible) says to tell it all to Him. It was His Word that pointed me in the right direction as a young child. The Word of God is a light for our steps, a lamp for our pathways, a plumb line for our thinking, and a sure compass for our souls. Without His Word our world would be doomed and our lives pointless, without hope in living and really no guidance for living the "good life."

TABLE OF CONTENTS

Part I: The Veiled Dawn—God's Dwelling: The Mennonite Life

Chapter 1   Palace Hall Landing 29
Realizing My Parents' Lives Are Dedicated to the Lord's Work.

Chapter 2   Open Skies Way 34
Reaching for the Stars at a Very Young Age.

Chapter 3   Shaded Days Path 41
My Head Is Covered with a Veil These Days

Chapter 4   Pure Water Run 49
My Eternal Pledge to Christ and the Church through Baptism

Chapter 5   Haunted Valley Way 53
After All the Punches and Weird Looks, I Kept My Faith

Chapter 6   Summer Glow Walk 57
Sharing My Love for God

Chapter 7   Sea Valley Way 60
Drowning in Loneliness

Chapter 8   Summer Flames Way 65
Hoping for a Fun-Filled Summer with Church Friends

Chapter 9   Evening Bird's Knoll 74
Enjoying the Summer Nights with the Family

Chapter 10   Mystic Dance Path........................... 78
Praying and Hoping My Mysterious Classmates Do Not Mess Up
Their One and Only Life.

Chapter 11   Spring Morning Run.......................... 82
My Visit to Lancaster Mennonite High School

Chapter 12   Garden Spot Place........................... 86
Enjoying My Friends in Lancaster, Pennsylvania

Chapter 13   Moonlighting Path 99
Summer Evenings with My First Love

Chapter 14   Falling Rain Way 104
My Fighting Spirit to Keep Jesus in My Life Has Lost Its Battle

**Part II (The Unveiled Dawn—The Worldly
Dwelling: My Life as a Non-Mennonite**

Chapter 15   Empty Song Place 117
My Worldly Friends and My Worldly Ways

Chapter 16   Stormy Hill Way........................... 122
Fatal Car Accident and Ann Marie's Wedding Day

Chapter 17   Distant Locks Way......................... 127
Saying Goodbye to My Parents Due to My Worldly Ways

Chapter 18   Broadway Path 131
Indulging in the Pleasures of the World

Chapter 19   Broken Land Way 138
Neglecting My Family Due to My New Lifestyle

Chapter 20   Summer Waves Place 143
Reconnecting with a School Friend from the Eighth Grade

Chapter 21   Low Tide Way 146
The Lowest Moments of My Life (Raped? Busted?)

Chapter 22   Scentless Way 154
The World Is Bittersweet—A Few Good Friends and a Few
Bad Friends

Chapter 23   Silken Leaf Way 164
Going Home for a Visit and Marriage Proposal

Chapter 24   Eternal Rings Way 171
My Wedding Day

Chapter 25   Snowdrift Downs 176
God Gives and Takes Away in One Breath

Chapter 26   Woodland Walk Path 179
Raising My Family in Our New Home

Chapter 27   Satellite Course 182
Trying to Hold on to My Position. Will I Win?

Chapter 28   Fallen Skies Way 186
Nervous Breakdown Is Looming on the Horizon

Chapter 29   Running Sand Knoll 193
Declaring I Will Run toward My Declared Instincts

Chapter 30   High Tide Path 204
New Relationship(s) Highs

Chapter 31   Cradle Rock Way 213
A Basket Case—a Crying Season

Chapter 32   Topsy-Turvy Place 221
My Upside Down World

Part III: The Good Life

Chapter 33   Honesty Way 229
Putting on My New Robe and Losing the Old Robe (My Old Identity)

Chapter 34   Glowing Days Pathway 236
Reconnecting with My Childhood Beau

Appendix I: My Inspiration for
a Fulfilling Life

Rise and Shine Way 245
Instructions for a Good Life 253

PART I

THE VEILED DAWN—
GOD'S DWELLING
THE MENNONITE LIFE

Chapter 1

PALACE HALL LANDING

Two years after I was born, my parents became very involved with mission work in 1957, reaching out to the Washington, D.C., and Baltimore suburbs and cities. They settled in Gaithersburg, Maryland, and were one of the founding families of the startup mission church, Gaithersburg Mennonite Mission Church. Their purpose in life was to make a difference in the community by bringing the unsaved to the Lord. Also it was my parents' desire to have a big family. They had been already blessed with three children, and Mom was expecting her fourth child. Richard, Ann Marie, and I were very excited about the new arrival of our new sibling in a few weeks.

Our family attended church on Sunday mornings, Sunday evenings, and Wednesday evenings. On Sunday afternoons we usually visited with families that would often come to our Sunday morning services. One Sunday afternoon Dad approached us and said, "Hey, my lovely family, let's go and visit with the new family that attended our service today!

Mom replied, "Honey I don't think we should visit so soon since we really don't know much about them!"

Dad gave Mom a big smile and said, "My dearest lady, beautiful wife, and loving mother with baby inside her womb, I feel God is in on this and I also know we will be welcomed since I am the two oldest boys' Sunday school teacher." Dad continued saying that one of the boys said he wishes his father would someday want to attend church with them.

I remember arriving at their house, and the garage door was open. I saw two oversized men without shirts on bent over two motorcycles. Their shorts were halfway down their bottoms. Dad approached them and said "Hello there! "They both were startled and very embarrassed since they jumped up and ran to the other side of the garage for their shirts. Dad continued saying, "We were just passing by and thought we would stop in to see if your boys would like to spend the day with our family at the Washington Grove playground?"

One of the men reached for Dad's hand and said, "I am Gene Harris, and who are you?" Dad answered back, "I am Adam Martin, your boys' Sunday school teacher. My wife Eva Lynn and children Richard, Ann Marie, and Sharon would love to have your boys come with us so we may be able to get a kickball game going.

Mr. Harris replied, "Adam, why don't we start the game in my backyard? I would like to play, also."

We all had so much fun that we did not want the game to end, but Mom whispered something in Dad's ear. Dad looked very surprised about the short whisper from Mom. Dad excitedly said "We are going to have a baby! We must leave now!"

As we were saying our goodbyes, Mr. Harris told dad that he will bring the boys to church next Sunday. I also heard Mr. Harris say to Dad, "Adam you are a genuinely nice guy, and now I know why my boys enjoyed their first Sunday school class today; it was because you were their teacher."

My father was very jovial and a lot of fun. He loved God, and he loved people and people loved him. I admired my parents. In my young eyes I thought they were perfect; they really cared about people. My mother radiated genuine warmth to the Mennonite community and the outside community. My parents practiced what they preached. I remember standing by their side after church meetings and listening to their conversations with other members or visitors. They showed so much kindness and love to all. They were my heroes.

Steve had made his appearance after midnight the next day. It was a long labor for Mom. When they finally brought my brother home, I would not leave his side since this was so exciting for me, having a baby living with us. I had been the baby for six years. Now I was a big sister enjoying every moment by his side, or holding him after Mom would nurse him which I thought was so disgusting, a baby sucking on Mom's breast. Mom would keep a diaper over his face so I couldn't see the feeding. Mom would allow me to burp him on occasion. He was so tiny but had big blue eyes when he opened them and a big nose for his little face. I was a proud big sister.

One day Dad brought a stranger home with him. Dad told us that Stan was homeless and had no family. Dad gave Stan a job and paid him well. He would eat dinner with us during the week, but on weekends he would leave and not return until Monday evenings. I remember one night for dinner Mom served us beef liver for dinner.

Stan disgustingly asked, "What is this mess?"

Mom replied, "You never had liver before?"

Stan jumped up from the table and mumbled, "Liver is for common people!" He left the room, and my parents seem very hurt over his comment. I was thinking to myself what does he mean by common people?

Richard spoke up after Stan was out of the house, "Dad now I understand why he has no one, he is a very nasty person. "

Dad still shaking his head over Stan's comment replied, "Yes, Richard, I agree, but we need to have Christ-love in our hearts for people like him. Hopefully someday he will have the love of Christ within him also."

A few months after living with us, Stan was in our back yard puffing on a white thing hanging out of his mouth. I asked him, "What are you puffing on?" He replied angrily, "It is called a cigarette!" He continued saying, "You need to run along!"

I thought to myself, I wonder what that thing tastes like. I was fascinated by the smoke coming out of his nose and mouth. If only I could find out. When he threw it on the ground and walked inside, I ran to it, picked it up and began puffing it. Nothing happened. No smoke came out of my mouth or nose. What did happen though, I was picked up by my father and was spanked and scolded and told that was wrong. We were both crying. I was sent to my room for the rest of the evening.

I was so confused about right and wrong. My parents were friends with people that had TVs, drank beer and liquor, smoked cigarettes, wore makeup and jewelry, yet we did not participate in any of those things. Not until I was almost seven years old did I finally realize who my parents were. They were missionaries, trying to be a witness to the world. Dad had a school bus that he used to bus children from outside our mission church community to Sunday school. Some Sundays I would ride with him to pick up the children and thought how lucky I was to have a caring parent as my dad. I was so proud of him. The children would run to the bus and have the biggest smiles on their faces. They would give Dad a big hug. Dad would lead the children in singing songs during our bus ride.

Most of the children's parents were not at all interested in attending our church or any church. Dad really cared about all the little children he picked up and he called them all by their name and always asked how they were doing.

I was in second grade when I was introduced to the cruel world. It was my seventh birthday. The teacher announced birthdays to the class. Sherry, the pretty blonde sitting next to me, stood up as the teacher called her name. The teacher then called my name, and I also stood up and the class sang "Happy Birthday."

After the song we sat down and Sherry snapped at me, "You are a copy cat. Today is not your birthday. You are a liar!"

Sherry did not talk to me after that day. I was so embarrassed of her actions toward me. She seemed like a spoiled kid. She always looked so pretty in her little matching outfits. All my classmates looked up to her since she was the prettiest girl in our class. I remember I was treated as an outcast, probably because my mother made my dresses. My dresses were long (below the knees), and I also wore braids. Actually the brown (colored) children were my friends; maybe because of their braids. They also were treated as outcasts.

My friend Stephanie smelled like a wood stove, but she was always very clean and had the most radiant smile. Her teeth were so perfect and so white; they reminded me of piano keys. Stephanie's many braids were tight and perfectly placed on her head. We would eat lunch together, and at recess we would hang out together. We shared our secrets with each other. She felt sad also that we were excluded from most of the groups of kids in our class.

One day I asked her if she attended a church. She replied, "Yes, I go with my grandmother every Sunday." She then took a deep breath, and I noticed her big sparkling eyes were welling up with tears. Stephanie continued saying, "I live with my grandmother, and I don't know my dad. My mother walked out on us about three years ago. We have not seen her since. We believe she is living on the streets (homeless). My grandmother says she has had a drug problem since she was fifteen years old."

I invited Stephanie to our Vacation Bible School and she accepted. Dad picked her up in the Sunday school bus. She had her little New Testament with her and a big smile on her face. Dad asked her, "Do you know the song "This Little Light of Mine?" She shouted "Yes!" My dad started singing and then the whole bus chimed in with us.

"This little light of mine, I'm going to let it shine. This little light of mine, I'm going to let it shine, let it shine, let it shine, let it shine. Shine all over Gaithersburg, I am going to let it shine, shine all over Gaithersburg, I'm going to let it shine, let it shine, let it shine, let it shine. Hide it under a bushel, *NO,* I'm going to let it shine. Hide it under a bushel *NO,* I'm going to let it shine, let it shine, let it shine, let it shine."

We were shining all over Gaithersburg that night. After Bible school Mom rode with us giving out little baggies of cookies. I thought to myself that night how blessed I was to have wonderful parents. They were so giving, so kind and really wanted to help out the less fortunate.

Chapter 2

OPEN SKIES WAY

It was a scorching August day, and there was not a cloud to be seen. The sky had an openness about it on the day we moved into our beautiful home my father and uncle had built in the suburbs of Gaithersburg. My mother was a stay-at-home mother (most Mennonite married women do not work outside the home), so we were very fortunate to have an awesome new home on an acre of land. Our house was surrounded by woods, and there was a creek not far from our backyard. We had no sidewalks and lived off a gravel road, named Rocky Road. The country air was filled with a manure smell from a nearby farm. The big maple and oak trees surrounding our house gave plenty of shade on this very warm day.

I was very excited about our new home in the country. My home for the first years of my life was in downtown Gaithersburg in a two-story house built in the early 1900s. There were many homes surrounding ours; there was also a beer/liquor store close by and a saloon about a block away. There was always excitement on our street since we had a lot of foot and automobile traffic. We could always see many people waiting for a ride at the bus stop outside our front door.

One evening about bedtime, I remember hearing noises coming from the front room of our house, which was used as an office. Dad was very concerned and thought someone had broken into our house. Dad told us to go upstairs to our bedrooms and lock our doors. I remember many times when drunken men would knock on our door asking to use our telephone. After the police left, Dad came upstairs and said, "I left the fan on, and the noise we were hearing was paper flying and hitting the wall." We all laughed.

I can remember many times when Mom would walk us to school in the mornings, and we would see men passed out by the roadside. Mom would say, "Children, this is what alcohol does to a person; it makes you really sleepy!" Of course, I believed her and said one day, "Mom, can we maybe talk to them about sleeping too much?"

Mom replied with a very sad look on her face. "Children, they are called homeless people; they have no home, and most of them are alcoholics." Mom continued, saying, "Stan was once homeless, but we gave him a home and a job and soon, if he stays away from the bottle, he will be moving out and hopefully have his own home and family someday. Let's keep Stan in our prayers every day, children, okay?"

Mom had been very concerned about her offspring seeing this way of life every morning and evening due to the saloon several doors down from our house. There were discarded beer bottles, many broken, alongside the road.

One morning as I was skipping along the sidewalk on my way to school, I lost my balance and fell on a broken beer bottle and slit my knee wide open. Blood gushed down my leg from two long, very deep cuts. I cried out, "Mom, I see my meat and bones!" Mom took her sweater off, wrapped it quickly around my knee, picked me up and ran home with me in her arms. At the hospital, I almost passed out when they took the sweater off my knee. One hour later, I had about fifty stitches in my knee.

Dad arrived at the hospital as we were leaving with balloons and a lollipop. He picked me up and said, "My dear little girl, I am so glad you still have your leg attached so we can skip together when you get all better!" We all laughed!

I was so proud of my Dad; he worked very hard; he was not at all lazy or sleepy like the men I saw on my street. He was a stone/brick mason by trade; working Monday through Saturday; sometimes fifteen-hour days. He never worked on Sunday, (our Sabbath day) the Lord's day. We believed the Lord's Day should be kept as a day of devotion and worship. Everyone in my family regularly attended church services and Sunday school unless we were not feeling well. Feasting and pleasure seeking were strictly avoided on Sundays. Secular business and labor were to be avoided as much as possible unless your occupation was a farmer or a doctor.

I guess Dad's hard work provided us with our new beautiful home, plus he was very gifted and talented when it came to designing and choosing the right material for the construction of our home. I remember that at the first event we had in our new home, people were in awe over our house. One of our guests commented, "There is a mansion waiting for us in Heaven but we have a mansion on earth, too." Dad just smiled and thanked her for the compliment.

I loved my bedroom, which I shared with my older sister Ann Marie (ten years old) who was two years older than I. The furniture was new, and my mother let Ann Marie and I select our bedding from a Pennsylvania Dutch Quilting Catalog. Mom also allowed us to select our wall colors. She wanted us involved with helping to decorate our new home.

Richard was twelve years old and had his own bedroom. Steve was almost two years old and had the smallest room. The reason why there was such an age gap between my younger brother and me was because my mother (pregnant at the time) was in a serious car accident when I was one year and one month years old and lost the baby, my sister Wanda Jean. She was stillborn. Mom carried her almost full term, nine months. Mom was seriously injured in the accident and was bedridden for a few months. I was told that my siblings and I were farmed out to my aunts and uncles for a couple of months.

September was approaching, and I was very excited about attending a new school since I had met some really cool kids in my neighborhood. We were blessed with nice neighbors, and my mom informed me that my church friend Donna will be attending my school. I was going into the third grade. Ann Marie was really nervous about attending the new school since she had many learning challenges. She struggled with reading and arithmetic. Finally, after much consideration, and many meetings with the principal, my parents were told Ann Marie would be placed in Special Ed classes.

The next few years were happy ones, with the arrival of more siblings, Keri and Dennis. Foster children would come and go. I was surrounded by children; children were everywhere. Our entertainment was playing a lot of board games. If it was a nice day, we would play outside with the neighbors—after the chores were done, of course. There was no television, but we did have a radio and record player.

I would spend most of my free time with my siblings and foster children, playing Sunday school. I would have them sit around our game table in the basement, and we would sing songs from a hymnal. Then I would read them a Bible story and give a quiz. The questions were usually true/false since some of them were only five years old. Ann Marie was challenged in reading, so I would encourage her to read aloud with me. I would help her with the pronunciation of the words. She would become very frustrated and leave upset. My brother Steve, soon to be five years old, listened well and always managed to have almost a perfect score on the quizzes.

One day Mom called me into the living room. She was sitting on the sofa with a big cardboard box in front of her and said, "Sharon, please come here; look here, I want you to take this catalog along with these boxes of cards to the neighbors and sell them to anyone who is interested in buying them." Mom continued, "You are great with people and with your big smile and loving personality, you will be a great salesperson; just don't give them away. The prices are listed on the back of the catalog."

I was so excited about making my own money. I was only ten years old. I could not wait for the weekend. After the first month of selling, Mom was very pleased. She would give me a percentage of every sale.

Mom did confide in me that she was struggling with meals. She did not have the money some weeks to buy groceries. I remember for many dinners Mom would serve us hot chocolate with white bread and apple butter. We also would have scrambled eggs for dinner sometimes because eggs were very cheap.

I noticed after selling door to door for a few months that many of my customers were asking me, "Are there any good sales going on right now?"

I replied back, "I will find out and let you know."

The next time I had a sign on the box, Buy one box of cards and the second one is fifty percent off. My sales doubled that month. One summer morning Mom announced to me that we received a letter from the American Card Company, advertising we were listed as number three in sales for June. Mom thought it would be great if we could be number one in sales for the month of July since I was out of school.

Mom would drive me into town. She would drop me off at 9:30 a.m. with a packed lunch and informed me that she would meet me at the Country Store at 4:00 p.m. I would go door to door, and most of the women that answered their door were so welcoming; some offered me cookies and milk. The first day, I was so full of cookies and milk that I didn't even open my lunch. I remember being so tired that I found a shady tree and fell sound asleep that afternoon. A dog awoke me by licking my lips. I am sure I had some cookie crumbs left on my mouth. At the end of the day, Mom totaled my sales and informed me that we were going to be number one for July if I kept selling like I I did that day!

Many of my customers wanted to know about me, my family, and my Mennonite background. They were very impressed with my sales pitch and my knowledge of my faith.

The entire month Mom would encourage me to be my best person: be kind, give compliments, and of course always try to get a sale at every house. At some homes, I would visit for eternity it seemed, but I did always leave with a sale. I think they got the hint that I wanted to sell them something before leaving.

I was also gifted in accessorizing rooms since I had done a lot of the interior decorating at my home. My catalog had a few pages of accessory items. I often suggested an item from the catalog if I thought something would add a final touch to a table or a fireplace mantel.

We were number one in July and August and again in November. I enjoyed selling and mostly I enjoyed visiting with my customers. I knew at a very young age that I liked people and people liked me. A lot of my customers were very impressed that I was selling door to door at such a young age.

I continued door-to-door selling for a couple of years until I was asked to babysit for my neighbors. That money was also pretty good. I was in big demand for babysitting and the children loved me since I would play board games, play hide and seek, and read and tell Bible stories. After tucking the children in for the night, I would clean house. When the cleaning was done, I would turn on the TV and watch *The Lawrence Welk Show*. I enjoyed his shows, watching couples waltz around in each other's arms. I knew that my parents would not be too happy about me watching TV.

One night after tucking the children into bed, I received a phone call from Joan, the mother of the children I was babysitting, asking me if I could spend the night since they had too much to drink and would not be home. I agreed I would. Joan said it was okay to sleep in their bedroom. I noticed the room was cluttered, so I started hanging up clothes and noticed the furniture needed dusting. As I was dusting the furniture, I picked up a book titled *How to Have the Best Sex with Your Spouse*. I started flipping through the pages and thought, "Holy Cow" is this what married couples do to each other? How disgusting, I thought. I wondered if my parents did that to each other, having oral sex.

The nights I babysat, I would miss our family devotions, something I looked forward to with the family. My parents were always trying to encourage us to read the Bible daily. They would always tell us the Bible is the best book for us all. Mom would play the piano while my Dad, my siblings, and I would sing. We would discuss our day and pray, thanking God for another wonderful day he had given us. As long as I can remember, as far back as five years old, Mom and Dad would fill my siblings and me with truths about the Bible. My mother's heart was filled with love for her children. She prayed for God's almighty strength and guidance to be a good role model to her offspring showing faith, love, patience, and meekness. As mentioned in I Timothy 6:12, "Your child's heart is at stake."

I remember Mom would start her day sitting by the big picture window in the living room with her Bible, feasting upon the Word. I am sure this quiet time with the Lord prepared her busy day for all the homemaking duties. She would graciously float through each day unruffled by stress and unbothered by the obstacles tossed her way. The clutter of toys, children running through the house, and all the gardening work and canning ahead of her did not seem to frazzle her. I saw firsthand her high calling to be the best Christlike mother to her family.

Chapter 3

SHADED DAYS PATH

The first day of middle school (seventh grade), I was awakened by Mom yelling, "Wake up, Sharon, it is time to get up! We have to fix your hair this morning." What she meant by "fix my hair" was putting my long hair up in a bun and covering it up with my custom-fitted covering, which the Mennonites refer to as a "covering."

I wanted to wear my ponytails, so I pleaded with my mother. "Please Mom let me wear my ponytails to school."

"No, Sharon," she replied in a stern voice.

I said, "Mom I don't think a bun is very becoming on me!"

Mom scolded back at me, "Sharon the way a person looks isn't as important as having a beautiful heart!"

As Mom was fixing my hair for school, I was trying to imagine what my worldly friends would say to me. I fussed loudly to my parents about wearing the cape to school, and finally my parents agreed to only wearing the cape to church and all church-related functions. l was allowed to wear a skirt and a blouse to school instead of the modest cape dress.

A cape dress is to hide your shape if you had any. There was this extra piece of fabric, which matched the dress and fitted over your shoulders, coming down to your waist in the front and back.

My mother was a very reasonable person, easy to talk to. She was doing her best to raise me and didn't have just me to contend with. I was, at this time, one of six children. Mom wanted me to be happy. She would let me pick out my fabrics and she sewed dress after dress for Ann Marie and me.

The coming Sunday Ann Marie and I would be joining the Mennonite Church, which means being baptized and obeying the Mennonite rules. I accepted Jesus as my Savior at age eleven. I was attending Camp Hebron, a church camp in Pennsylvania. I remember that night so vividly. The setting in the mountains was awesome. The other campers and I were seated around a huge bonfire. The fire was blazing, and the guest speaker was lecturing from Acts 17:29-31:

> Therefore since we are God's offspring, we should not think that the divine being is like gold or silver or stone—an image made by man's design and skill. In the past God overlooked such ignorance but now he commands all people everywhere to repent. For he has set a day when He will judge the world with justice, by the man He has appointed. He has given proof of this to all men by raising Jesus from the dead.

The minister explained to us that someday Jesus (God's son) will be returning to earth, and we should be ready to enter an eternity of glory and blessedness. We can enter Heaven only by accepting Jesus as our Savior and repenting of all our sins. I thought to myself, "I don't want to miss out on Heaven and spend eternity in hell."

I remember at one of our revival meetings a year before that I left one night, afraid that I might go to hell if I didn't accept Jesus as my Savior. I could not sleep that night since all I could think about was spending eternity in Hell. "Hell is darkness, a place of torment, prepared for the devil and his angels where with them. The wicked will suffer the vengeance of eternal fire forever and ever" preached the hellfire-and-brimstone revival minister. I did not want to spend eternity with Satan and bad people. The next night I remember Richard along with a very close friend accepting Jesus as their Savior; they were fourteen years old.

After the sermon, our camp pastor invited us to raise our hand if we would like to invite Jesus into our hearts. I think that night about fifteen of us raised our hands. We wept with joy and sang around the campfire until we could not keep our eyes open. One of the songs we sang I remembered singing in our revival meetings often:

O victory in Jesus, my Savior, forever!
He sought me and he bought me with his redeeming blood!
He loved me ere I knew Him, and all my love is due Him,
He plunged me to victory beneath the cleansing flood.

I remember going to sleep that night feeling safe and loved because Jesus was in my heart. I felt like a new person; I had so much happiness within me. I had so many new things I wanted to learn about my newfound faith.

The next day I was witnessing to a few African American girls from New York that I had met in my Bible study class (I enjoyed hanging out with them since they were always so happy and enjoyed playing pranks on each other). I shared my experience with them about accepting Jesus as my Lord and Savior. I explained to them when you ask Jesus into your heart, He will wash all your sins away, and He will become the ruler in your life. I discussed with them that through Jesus living in our hearts, we will have peace, love, joy, and patience—everything to have a beautiful life. They also accepted Jesus, and thanked me for sharing my newfound faith with them. At that time I knew my calling was to let everyone know about Jesus. I did not want anyone to miss eternal life with God.

When I returned from camp, I reached out to Ann Marie, asking her if she would like to receive Jesus in her heart, and I explained to her about being ready to go to Heaven when she dies and that if she were to die right now, she would not make it to Heaven. Ann Marie accepted Jesus as her Savior, and I led her in prayer, asking God to help her always to be the best person she can be, like Jesus, and also be a witness to her friends.

Well, my hair was finally up, and I looked into the mirror and frowned at the plain girl frowning back at me in the mirror. I knew my new look will not be accepted well by my school friends. I felt and looked ten years older. I was twelve years old. You see, my hair was my biggest attribute. It was long, straight, and blonde. I have dark eyebrows with hazel eyes and freckles. I was very popular in grade school with my church friends and neighborhood friends alike. I wanted everyone to like me. I wanted to share my kindness everywhere I went, creating happiness in everyone's day.

I went outside and walked up and down my driveway, feeling scared and nervous inside. As I stood in the driveway under our big shade tree waiting for the bus, I said a little prayer, "Please God, help my friends accept the new me, and please keep me shaded from all the wrong looks I may get from them."

The bus ride was very long. We had to ride for an hour or longer it seemed. The bus chugged out of Laytonsville and lurched around the winding country roads, picking up kids here and there. The windows were down, letting the fresh country air blow through the bus. It was a bright, sunny morning with not a cloud in the sky. The children were unusually quiet. It seemed like all eyes were on me. I sat alone wondering if any of my school friends getting on would sit with me. I knew I was going to be the only Mennonite girl in school. Ann Marie was attending another school due to her learning disabilities. There were a few Mennonite boys, but they looked pretty ordinary, which seemed unfair.

As the bus drove up to the school I could feel my throat tightening and my hands began to tremble. I was too scared to get off the bus. I waited until everyone was off the bus before getting up. As I walked to the front of the bus, the bus driver introduced himself to me. "Hello young lady," he said, "I'm Mr. Bell, and what is your name?"

I answered very softly, "My name is Sharon."

He then smiled at me and said, "Sharon, don't look so sad—it's going to be just fine and you have a beautiful smile!"

As I got off the bus I turned to him and gave him a big smile and thanked him for the compliment. Well, he did make me feel a little more comfortable about school.

As I walked into the school office to pick up my schedule, I noticed a few of my friends from grade school. As I approached Susan, a friend from sixth grade, she turned her back to me and started talking to a girl standing next to her. I thought to myself that I was an embarrassment to her, so I found my schedule in the stack of papers and hurried out of the office.

My homeroom class was at the other end of the school. I'm going to be late on my first day of school, I thought to myself, so I began walking fast and then even faster when I heard someone yell behind me, "Hey, you with the white net, there's no running in the halls," and then I heard laughter as my eyes filled with tears. I felt so embarrassed. I tried not to cry but tears started streaming down my face.

My grandmother warned me that I was going to stand out because of my covering and modest dress. She told me to ignore any demeaning actions from my classmates and to just pray that they would accept me for who I am. "Sharon, you can be a witness to them by showing them that you have God's love in your heart," she added. Also she reminded me to forgive the ones that do me wrong.

My grandmother was a very kind and humble lady. Her ancestors emigrated from Switzerland to America in the 1700s and settled in Lancaster, Pennsylvania. My grandmother's family bought a huge farm in Hagerstown, Maryland, in 1880 and lived there until she moved to Colorado at age eighteen to help out in a Sanitarium Hospital for a few years. She then moved to California to work for a famous Jewish family, doing their laundry and cooking.

My grandmother met my grandfather at Niagra Falls, Canada, in 1928 and married him a year later. She was twenty-nine years old, and my grandfather was thirty-six years old. She moved to

Canada where she and my grandfather raised five children until he succumbed to colon cancer; he was only forty-eight years old. My grandfather's people were Old Ordered Mennonites. They were often mistaken for Amish people since their transportation was horse and buggy. My grandmother lost the farm in Canada, and her children were taken from her since she could not provide for them. They were distributed among the relatives. My father was only eight years old when his father died. He then moved in with his uncle and aunt who had a farm in Hagerstown, Maryland.

I always enjoyed my visits with my grandmother Hettie. She had so many stories to tell about her life experiences. Her first job was working at the sanitarium in Colorado. Apparently she was a prankster. She would put dead mice under bed pillows of her coworkers. One night she got into her own bed and put her hands under her pillow and felt something furry; she screamed, "What is that?" waking up the whole sanitarium. Someone had played the same joke on her. After that there were no more mice pranks.

Grandma Hettie also shared many stories about working for a very famous Jewish family, Mr. and Mrs. Silvers in Los Angeles, California. She told me she had learned so much from them. Living with them was very educational, she would say. My grandmother learned many skills from them since she only had a sixth grade education. Also the Jewish family learned patience and kindness from my grandmother. She reminded them to put their complete trust in God. My grandmother would often say to me, "Remember to always be kind to people even if they are unkind to you. God will always bless and take care of his children." She often reminded me that if God is with you, he will shade you from all evil.

The bell rang as I was stepping into my first class. I took a seat at the back of the room. I could feel myself trembling as I completed the forms left on top of the desk. I was the first one to complete the forms so I glanced at the kids around me. The girls looked so pretty with their long, flowing hair hugging their shoulders, and some of the girls had short hair with lots of waves. A few of them had on white boots with little skirts.

The boys were dressed just like the Mennonite boys—their hair was maybe a little longer than the Mennonite boys'.

The teacher was an older lady with short gray hair, and she had a lot of heavy jewelry on. She noticed I had completed the forms so she began walking towards me saying, "You're done already? Are you sure you completed everything?"

"Yes," I replied.

She picked up my forms and glanced at them, "Wow, she said, you have beautiful handwriting!"

I smiled at her, thanking her.

"And you have a beautiful smile, Sharon," she whispered.

The bell rang. It was the bell for second period. I gathered my things and hurried out into the hallway and looked for the stairs. I had to go to the second floor where the English classes were. As I was going up the stairs, I noticed a few boys were standing at the bottom of the stairs looking up the girls' skirts and giggling to each other, commenting on their underwear. I thought to myself, how disgusting! I had never seen such awful gestures! My dress was below the knee so I continued climbing the stairs holding my dress close to me.

The bell rang as I took my seat. The teacher was very pretty, with long, blonde hair and beautiful blue eyes. She looked so young. We made eye contact with each other and nodded our heads. She walked over to me and reached for my hand. She cupped her hands over my hand and said, "Welcome to my class. I know you will be a wonderful student; I know the Mennonites. They are very kind people." She continued to say, "If you ever need anyone to talk to about anything, please keep me in mind." I felt like a million dollars after I left her class.

The first day didn't really seem so bad, I thought to myself, as the last bell rang indicating school was over. As I picked up my things and hurried out to find my bus, I saw a group of my church guy friends from Goshen Mennonite Mission Church huddled in a circle. I walked over to them and asked, "Hey, how are you guys doing?" They totally ignored me and walked the other way to their buses. It was so hurtful that they acted like they didn't know me. I was even an embarrassment to my church friends, I thought to myself as I looked for my bus.

I found my bus and found an empty row of seats. I cried most of the way home. I felt so alone.

Chapter 4

PURE WATER RUN

Today was a big celebration for me, my family, and my church friends. There were four young believers, including Ann Marie, joining the Mennonite church after Sunday school.

I was so excited about getting ready for church. I was wearing my newly made cape dress. I had my hair up in a bun and was just putting on my new white covering, when Mom walked into the bathroom and asked Ann Marie and me if we needed any help putting on our coverings. She had some straight pins in her hands and she secured our covering to our hair with the pins.

"It is very windy out there today, my dear girls, and I don't want you to be chasing your coverings in your beautiful dresses," Mom softly said as she gave us a big hug. Mom continued saying, "Girls, I am so proud of you for your decision to become Mennonites. You know the rules and disciplines that you were taught in the Instruction classes. You will need to abide by those rules at all times; there are no exceptions."

Of course we nodded our heads to confirm that we now know what is right from wrong after attending the classes every Thursday evening for two months. While in our Instruction classes, I was very concerned about Ann Marie's reading abilities. She was even struggling with very simple words. She was now almost fourteen years old, and I was helping her with all the words when it was her turn to read from our Instruction book. I thought to myself whether she was being taught anything at the school she was attending for special needs children? I thought this special school was going to help her learn more than a regular school. At least that is what Mom had told me.

After Sunday school, Ann Marie and I, along with the others to be baptized, were asked to sit on the front pew. The bishop talked to us and the congregation about being baptized. He stressed to us about humility and trust, the honor and sanctity of the Mennonite Church and the meaning of commitment. He gently said, "You are about to make a promise before your sisters and brethren in Christ, and it is a holy vow that will bind you for the rest of your life. To break this vow is a very serious thing. Are you ready for this commitment?"

We all nodded our heads and said "Yes!"

The congregation sang a few songs, followed by a baptism sermon. After closing his sermon, the bishop stepped down from the pulpit, picked up a cup of water, and walked over to us. He poured water on my head while saying my name, "Sharon, I baptize you in the name of the Father and of the Son and of the Holy Spirit, Amen." My eyes began filling up with tears, and then I began crying tears of happiness. I was immersed with the Holy Spirit. I have Jesus with me now and always. Following the baptism, many members of the congregation walked up front and welcomed us into the Mennonite fold. I received my first Holy Kiss, actually many Holy Kisses from my now "Sisters in Christ."

Thanksgiving was approaching and I was looking forward to having a break from school. Mom had been preparing for the traditional family gathering at our house. We were having about forty people (all family) this year. My best friends these days were my cousins. A few of my aunts, uncles, and cousins were at my baptism, but I was so looking forward to seeing them again and sharing with them my joy of being a Mennonite. My favorite female cousin

Deidre had also just joined her Mennonite church in Chambersburg, Pennsylvania, and we were looking forward to sharing our experiences with each other. I would share most of my secrets with her. Deidre was one year older than me.

On Thanksgiving Day we had a full house. All of my aunts and uncles with my cousins arrived early. My cousins and I started a softball game. After dinner we gathered around the piano and sang hymns until it was time to say goodbye. We had a very happy extended family. It was so hard to say our goodbyes since I knew it would be another year before we would have a gathering like this again.

It was Sunday night after Thanksgiving, and I was preparing for Monday. I still had some English homework to do for class tomorrow. I always looked forward to my English class. We were reading "A Christmas Carol" by Charles Dickens. What a great story about doing the right thing makes you feel better. One day, Mrs. Wright asked the class, "Who is interested in doing the hallway bulletin board from one of the scenes in the book?" I raised my hand and immediately was told I had the assignment.

That night Mom drove me to the art store to purchase colored construction paper and other necessary material. I worked every night on the scene and was not getting very far with it. Dad saw that I was getting very discouraged (he was blessed with great drawing skills) so he offered to help me. We worked together every evening after dinner for about a week. As Dad drew the scenes, I would cut and paste. Our last night working on the scene, Dad gathered the family around the table and we sang Christmas carols until it was time to go to bed.

Dad ended our day by praying, "Dear Lord thank you for all Your bountiful blessings. Thank you for our wonderful children who are so special to Mom and me; they bring us so much joy and happiness. Please keep us safe and sound as we sleep in peace tonight in our beautiful home that you have blessed us with, In Jesus' name, Amen."

Dad drove me to school the next day with my completed project. He helped me staple the scene onto the hall bulletin board outside my English class. As we were working on the bulletin board, my teacher walked up to us and said "Wow, what an awesome job!" She was very impressed and I was also impressed with my dad's creative abilities.

I remember many Sunday mornings he would leave for church earlier than the rest of the family to draw scenes from the Bible on the blackboard pertaining to the sermon. My father definitely had a gift and I was so proud of him! Dad was quite impressed with the scene when he applied the last staple. Dad asked me, "Sharon, could you bring the book home so I can read the "Christmas Carol" story?"

"Sure Dad," I replied.

He loved the story and said, "Always remember, Sharon, doing good things will improve your life!" He added, "The Bible tells you that also, and you know Sharon, when we stand on the truth of the scriptures in God's Word, we are on solid ground, not quicksand, and we will have a very strong foundation for life."

Chapter 5

HAUNTED VALLEY WAY

The first few months in middle school seemed endless. I was horrified of what I was seeing and hearing from my classmates—what a scary world. I ate my lunch alone most days, unless my church friend Donna joined me. She was not a Mennonite but lived with Mennonites who cared for foster children. Donna was eight years old when her father died of a heart attack; he was only thirty-eight years old. A few months after her father died, her mother was in a serious car accident, which left her almost an invalid. Donna and her siblings were put in foster care.

Donna and I became best friends in elementary school. Her Mennonite foster parents made her wear skirts or dresses below the knee. She had to wear her beautiful long silk black hair in two ponytails. Her olive complexion accented her deep chestnut brown eyes. I thought she had the most beautiful face. We spent most of the summer together camping, having slumber parties, and attending youth outings.

"Hey, Sharon, may I join you?" Donna asked.

"Oh, I would love that," I replied.

"I'm so sorry if I've hurt your feelings Sharon," Donna whispered, "but I met a really cool girl in my history class, and she always invites me to have lunch with her and her friends." Donna continued, "Sharon, I'm so sorry that you're so different now. You used to be outgoing, bubbly, and full of energy, but you've changed." Donna continued on to say, "I think it's high time you start enjoying life again." Donna was hiking up her skirt and, if she wore a dress, a belt was added so she could shorten the length.

I always sought to please others so I began putting a plan together how I could make friends. I knew in the back of my mind that my classmates thought I was just so different from them. They had no desire to give me a chance to know them. The next period was math class and we were having a quiz. I overheard a conversation in class the day before that Becky a beautiful, popular girl was not getting it. Her desk was next to mine. I hurried to class and I noticed she had her book opened. I sat down and whispered to her, "Do you need help with anything?"

Becky looked up with tear-filled eyes and cried, "I'm going to flunk this quiz." So I began explaining to her how to solve the equations that we were to be quizzed on.

She thanked me and said, "Sharon, you are a godsend!" During the quiz, I placed my answers on my desk so Becky could see and copy if she needed to.

Becky walked with me to the next class. "Sharon," Becky said, "why do you wear that white cap and the longer dresses?"

I replied, "I'm a Mennonite, and Mennonites believe in covering their head at all times and that our clothing should be very modest and simple."

That night in bed I thought about what Donna said to me at lunch—how I've changed. I used to be so happy and outgoing, but now I had become very shy and quiet. The reason why I was so quiet and kept to myself was that I felt I was an embarrassment to my friends because of my appearance. I thought about the insane comments George in my science class would make about my head covering. He asked me one day if he could borrow my net for fishing. I was so embarrassed since the entire class heard his comment. George would often toss spit balls at me when the teacher was not watching, trying to hit my covering. One day I felt something hit my covering, and I turned around to say something to him and in the back row I saw a sad face on Ally, one of my classmates. The expression on her face never left me that day.

I was exhausted tonight so my bedtime prayer was short and sweet as I asked the Lord to forgive George for his meanness to me. I did not look forward to school much since I was constantly being teased about my head covering.

Several months passed by and summer was approaching. I was looking forward for the school year to end. I received awards for perfect attendance, track and field, and an Honor Roll award. My favorite classes were English and Physical Education. In English class my essays were often read by the teacher. She would tell the class that they should take lessons in creative writing from me. In my physical education class, although I had to wear my dress, I was the fastest sprinter. I was not allowed to take a shower. Thank God it was my last period. I also really enjoyed gymnastics; it was so exciting and new to me. Although I was fully dressed (dress to the knees), I was allowed to wear a pair of shorts under my dress.

I remember asking Mom for $10.00 at the beginning of the school year so I could purchase a gym suit, and she responded immediately, "No Sharon that is being worldly, and we are not of the world. We are to set an example, not be like them."

"But Mom, please let me buy a gym suit," I begged.

"Why would you want to do that?" she said sternly.

"Because I could run even faster without my dress getting in the way, and I could participate better in gymnastics," I answered.

"Sharon, I'm very disappointed in you," and she added in a trembling voice, "Sharon, your legs are to be covered, not to show the world." I really felt so bad about disappointing my mother since her love for me and my siblings was so deep. I would always try to please her. She was definitely my best friend and role model.

I remember my first time on the trampoline, up, up and away I went. I thought I was going to touch the ceiling with my hands. I did not want to stop doing all the fun exercises. I saw a few classmates whispering and laughing to one another and pointing to me. I am sure they were talking about my dress billowing out and some-times covering my face. I expect it was a hilarious sight.

Many things about the Mennonites were good, but sometimes I wondered if I would be happier if I were not a Mennonite. I prayed to God that night asking for help in my struggles about being so different and feeling so lonely. I asked God to strengthen me on my journey with Him. I ended my prayer saying, "Please carry me, Lord, through this valley of loneliness, Amen." I so wanted to please God, Mom and Dad, and my church family.

I woke up the next morning feeling very happy and cheerful knowing today was the last day of school. There was a chill in the air so I grabbed a sweater and stepped outside. The morning air was considerably cool, and a chill shivered through me. As I approached the bus stop Ann Marie, Richard, and the neighbors were lining up for the bus. I sat alone and asked God to forgive me for doubting my faith. I wanted to be a witness to the world, and I actually enjoyed sharing my love for God to nonbelievers. I made up my mind to serve God to the fullest, no matter what comes against me because I know God will honor me and prepare me for any of the difficult challenges I am facing.

Chapter 6

SUMMER GLOW WALK

Summer was finally here and school was forgotten. I spent the summer having fun with my Mennonite friends. Our having fun was hanging out at youth meetings and attending a church camp. I looked forward to our youth outings, which consisted of having picnics, playing softball, and taking hikes on mountain paths.

The pastor of my church asked a few of us young people to participate in a door-to-door witness canvassing. I was assigned several streets within walking distance from the church. The weather was warm when I began. It soon became very hot; maybe in the upper eighties. I was very thirsty for water, but I was so excited about the possibility of sharing my love for Jesus to nonbelievers that I ignored my thirst for water. As I approached the first house, I saw an older woman sweeping her sidewalk. I stopped a few feet from her and asked her, "Do you have any kind of spiritual belief?"

She replied, "I'm Catholic and a very devout Catholic!"

Smiling I said, "I would like to invite you to my church this Sunday. Services begin at 11:00 a.m. It's the Mennonite Church on Mills Road. We would love to see you there and bring your husband." As I handed her a tract (literature on "Finding Hope"), she asked me if I enjoyed witnessing.

Grinning, I replied, "I don't want anyone missing Heaven!"

As I continued walking, children were playing hopscotch in the street, one of my favorite games. They asked me if I would like to join in the next game, but I declined. There was no answer at the second and third houses so I left a pamphlet in the door. I approached a dead end but there was a big colonial house sitting back off the street with many cars in the driveway. As I got closer I could hear loud voices coming from the house. I knocked a few times before the door opened. Standing in the doorway was this big, burly white guy with hair to his shoulders. He smelled like smoke and liquor. I introduced myself and asked him, "Do you know Jesus?"

Slurring his words he replied, "I do not believe in Jesus."

So I said to him, "If you died today, where would you go? Do you believe in heaven or hell?"

He snapped back and said he didn't have time to discuss this nonsense and slammed the door in my face. I never experienced anything like that before. I never knew people could be so nasty. As I turned away from the door, a woman yelled at me from the window above, "Don't bother us again—stay away from our house." My head felt like it dropped to my knees. I was devastated. I wanted to run, but I found a shady tree and fell to the ground and cried. After a few minutes, I jumped up and continued on my way. It was getting late so I decided to leave the remaining tracts inside the mailboxes instead of knocking on doors.

The next day, I was busy packing, getting ready for camp. Dad was planning to take a car load of my church friends to camp in a few days. Our days at camp were spent hiking, horseback riding, swimming, softball, Bible study, and putting on skits. I met many new friends from all walks of life. This was a church mission camp, so there were many kids from broken homes. Some had abusive and alcoholic parents. Some of the stories I heard were dreadful. I thanked God many times for godly parents. Camp felt like paradise, but the threat of going back to school was looming on the horizon.

My mother had been busy making a couple of new dresses for my new school year, which was a few days away. I asked Mom if she could add some belt loops so I could wear a belt around my waist.

Her reply was, "Sharon, we are not to be showy."

I was often reminded by my parents how important it was to dress modestly. "You need to respect yourself, and people will see that you are different from the world. They will have respect for you," Mom would say. I always wanted to do what was right, and I totally did not have a problem with modest dressing just because I did not want the boys to be attracted to me physically. My parents drilled into me that immodest clothing sends the wrong message to boys. I remembered the first day of school in the seventh grade, the boys were looking up the dresses of girls as they were taking the stairs, and I was so thankful I had a dress that covered me below the knees. I didn't want anyone looking at my panties and I surely didn't want to tempt the boys to look up my dress.

One evening after I completed my chores and homework, I slipped outside to shoot some baskets with my neighbor friend, Billy. It was beginning to get dark, and as I was saying goodbye to my friend, he ran up to me and asked me if I would help him pick flowers for his mother. I, of course agreed and we walked into the field across from my house and started picking flowers, when suddenly, Billy threw me to the ground and he put his elbows on my arms and started humping me.

I yelled at him, "Let me up; what are you doing?" I was using my hips trying to get him off me but he was much bigger than me. He kept on humping until finally he took a couple of deep breaths. He got up and I ran frantically to the house, going straight to my room in tears. Why did that happen? I thought to myself. I was only twelve and Billy was thirteen. I was too embarrassed to tell Mom because I really didn't know how to explain what had happened. I avoided him after that encounter. I often thought, though, how good it felt, so I began experimenting with my pillow. I would hump my pillow as often as I could. What an awesome feeling.

Chapter 7

SEA VALLEY WAY

My fears soon became reality again. It had been two months into the eighth grade. Kids would pass me in the hallway and stare at me like I was from another planet. My mother agreed to allow me to wear a gym suit this year just because she knew how much I wanted to excel in gym. My gym teacher wrote a comment on my last progress report that if I wore a gym suit I could perform better and that I had great potential to be the best.

Several months went by as I was totally ignored by most of the kids except for a few African American girls in gym class. I couldn't wait to go home to cry in private. I despised school. I had noticed many different cliques this year, and I was the only one in my clique. I had no one to talk to or laugh with until my last period, gym class. I was drowning in a sea of tears and sadness. I felt like a lost boat at sea with no help in sight. My saving grace was my wonderful neighborhood friends who treated me as a normal human being.

A few months passed by and one day in gym class, Becky (she was the classmate that I helped in math last year) came over to me and asked me if I would like to join her and her friends. She and her friends were cheerleaders; actually they were the prettiest girls in school, I thought. They seemed so full of energy and were always laughing.

"Sharon," Becky said, "these are my friends, Ally (I remembered Ally from my science class last year) Joy, Deanne, and Betsy, and we would like to know how long is your hair?"

I replied, "I can almost sit on it. I've never cut my hair—it is against my religion."

"Can you maybe tomorrow let it down, and if I bring in one of my dresses and a pair of my go-go boots, would you maybe dress up for us?" Ally asked.

"Your parents will never know," Becky added.

My reply was, "God will see me, and I don't want to disappoint God." I continued to tell them that I know God is watching everything I do, and He knows how lonely I am, not having any friends to talk to at school. I opened my pain and I poured out my heart, and as I looked around I saw red, teary eyes. One by one the girls came over and hugged me. The remainder of the year was less painful. I looked forward to gym class since it was the last period and also I enjoyed sports. We were learning archery which was something I had never been exposed to. After a week into archery, I was in line getting ready to shoot my arrow, when I felt something hit me in the back of my head. I turned my body around to see a very thin-framed pretty girl with long blonde hair running toward me.

As I put my hand on my head covering I heard "I'm sorry, I didn't mean to, it was an accident", cried the girl running toward me. I had been shot with an arrow. Thank God for my bun. For the next few moments I heard not a sound. I managed to laugh, though I wanted to cry. The classmate that accidentally shot me was very apologetic and in tears.

She asked me, "Are you okay?"

I replied, "My bun saved my life," and I chuckled.

She said with her hand reaching out to me, "I'm Patty and so sorry we had to meet this way."

"I'm Sharon and new at this, so maybe we can learn together."

She asked me, "What grade are you in?"

I replied, "Eighth grade."

"I'm in ninth grade," Patty added.

Patty became my gym friend. She was very personable and a very kind girl. We would chat about our families, and she had many questions about the Mennonites. She was raised Catholic and attended Catholic school through the eighth grade. She did mention that she didn't have many friends since this year was her first year attending a public school. She asked me if I had to sleep with my covering on since I told her I had to wear it at all times. I said the only time my covering can come off is when I have to wash my hair and that's about twice a week. I chuckled and said," Just kidding."

Patty had never heard of or seen Mennonites before, but in one of our conversations she said her teachers (nuns) were very modest and wore habits and had to keep their heads covered also. She said she could never be a nun because they were not allowed to have husbands. Patty and I would talk about some day having a big family since we both come from large families. Patty had nine brothers and sisters.

Patty and I became lunch friends also. One day she asked me if I could maybe go home with her after school sometime, saying that her mother would love to meet me. My mother did not think it was a good idea since she didn't know Patty and her parents. We did exchange phone numbers the last day of school. We promised each other that we would stay in contact during the summer. She was going to high school next year so I was pretty sad about not being able to see her upon my return to school.

Summer was just around the corner and my parents were planning to become foster parents again. They were notified by social services that two sisters would be joining our family the last day of school. Upon their arrival, Mom informed Ann Marie and me that we would have to share our bedroom with them. Their first day was very emotional for them. They missed their brothers. Jackie was the older sister and confided in me the first night at bedtime about her family.

I asked her, "Jackie, why are you in foster care?"

She replied, "My mother threatened to kill me and my siblings. She was full of deep rage one day and chased us with an axe, but thankfully my father arrived home from work and calmed her down."

I noticed her eyes welling up with tears. I got out of bed and put my arms around her, and I told her how sorry I was that she had to live like that, being scared of her mom.

She told me that her dad was an alcoholic and could not keep a job and some days he would stay in bed all day. I was horrified at the stories she was telling me; how could parents be like that? I could not relate to it since I was very fortunate to have caring, loving parents. After the first week, Mom came into our room and asked Jackie and Pam if they would like to visit their mother at Sykesville Mental Institution.

Jackie replied anxiously, "Yes, I would love to. Can Sharon go with me?"

That Saturday Mom drove Jackie, Pam, and me to the hospital. I was nervous, not really knowing what to expect. The visit was very short, maybe ten minutes. I saw a very sad and disturbed woman. Jackie's mother was crying for most of our visit. Mom tried to comfort her and told her we were praying for her and that she would take care of her girls until she was able to again. Mom reminded her as we were leaving, "God loves you unconditionally, and you have been forgiven for your dangerous actions toward your children."

My mother always gave encouragement to the families that were brought in from the community. She would encourage the women to build up their families daily. She would refer to 1 Thessalonians 5:11; Hebrews 3:13, 12:1; and Romans 15:5. "Help them identify and get rid of everything that hinders them and entangles them. Challenge them to run with endurance the race of life that I've already marked out for them. Give them encouragement and pray for them."

I noticed at a very young age that Mom had many friends. When I was around her interacting with our neighbors, she was always kind, encouraging them to be the best parents, energizing them to get a lot done within a day. She was always baking and giving her cakes to the neighbors. Mom had a gift of giving; she had a heart of unselfishness. I heard a neighbor ask Mom one day, "How can you give so much?"

Mom replied back, "I can't help it, God has blessed me with the gift, and I just feel it's the right way to live."

She also had a listening ear when they needed comforting. It was Mom's desire to help mothers with challenging marriages to turn to God for guidance. I often heard her say, "It's only through Jesus we can conquer the foe and be victorious. In ourselves, without Jesus, we are the most miserable creatures."

Chapter 8

SUMMER FLAMES WAY

My new foster sisters and I would start our days early. We wanted to get our chores out of the way so we could play with the neighbors. Whenever I had alone time I would slip away to my room and lock the door. I would get my favorite pillow and begin humping. One day as I was humping my pillow, I thought of God watching me; He does see everything. After that thought, it was all over with the humping. I prayed to God asking him to heal me of this addiction.

There was no television in our home since that was definitely against our religion. We did have a radio and I would listen to WRBS every Saturday morning as I cleaned the house. WRBS was a Christian station and, at 9:00 a.m., a program called Christian Family Life aired daily. I looked forward to this program since the stories were so interesting and comforting to me. Most of the stories were about children living in troubled homes and suffering from parents who did not know the Lord. In time the parents would come to know the Lord, and finally the children felt truly loved by their parents.

I thanked God every day that I was being raised in a loving Godly home. My heart was filled with gratitude to have been blessed with godly parents who were devoted to the work of Christ. They were stable and did not bend to the ways of the world. I also noticed that their conduct and speech was so different from the world. I never saw them angry, and I never heard bad, disgusting words coming from their mouths.

It was time again to pack for church camp. This year Carol, my neighbor friend, planned on going with me. I was excited about camp this summer since I had a crush on a nice Mennonite boy from Lancaster, Pennsylvania. I was looking forward to seeing him again. I was thirteen years old and had just started my period. I felt really grown up and my hormones were kicking in. I was attracted to boys, and I wanted to have a boyfriend, so I was on a mission that week to spend a lot of time with Jake, the Lancaster boy. My cabin friend, Marsha showed me different ways to wear my hair up. I learned how to do a French twist.

The first evening after devotions, Jake approached me and said, "Wow! Sharon, you look gorgeous with that twist on your head." Of course, my veiling was covering most of the twist. His eyes were studying me as he continued to say, "Sharon, will you be my date to the banquet tomorrow night?"

I gave him a big grin and said, "Of course, I would be happy to be your date."

The next evening Jake walked over to my cabin, and we walked hand in hand to the banquet. We spent a lot of time together that week. I felt so comfortable and liked by him. Our last evening of camp, he walked me to my cabin and of course, we were holding hands. As we approached my cabin, he squeezed my hand and bent down and kissed me on the cheek saying, "Sharon, I really enjoyed this week with you. I think you are the most beautiful, nicest girl I ever met in my life. Plus you are so funny. I love to hear you laugh!"

I said smilingly, "I think you are the most handsome boy and I love your haircut! I am going to miss you and your hands." Actually, Jake was the first guy I had ever held hands with. He had really strong hands. We said goodnight.

That night I lay awake, feeling that I do belong to this world, and that I was the luckiest girl on earth to be friends with the best looking boy at camp. I finally felt happiness in my heart again. I felt like singing!

Back at home, I looked forward to the afternoons when the chores were done, and I could play with my friends in the neighborhood. I spent a lot of time with my best friend Carol. She had a brother Darren, who was a very good friend with Richard. The four of us would hang out with the other children in the neighborhood playing softball, basketball, kickball, and climbing trees. There were some really big, mature trees in our neighborhood, which I would climb to get away from my younger siblings. As I was climbing a big tree one day and hoping no one would see how ridiculous I looked with a dress on, I thought how nice it would be to have on a pair of my brother's trousers. It certainly would make climbing a bit easier.

Sitting on the top limb, I could see Richard and Darren bicycling toward me. As I lowered myself to the limb below me, I lost my grip on the limb above and fell, getting my dress caught on a branch. I could see I was bleeding. As I tried to get my dress loose, I heard Richard and Darren at the foot of the tree.

"Hey, Sharon, do you want to play softball? We are starting a game in ten minutes," shouted Richard.

"Yes, I would love to, but I'm caught on a branch and I can't get loose," I said nervously.

With Darren's hands cupped around his mouth, he yelled, "Sharon, I'll lend you a hand." As Darren was climbing up the tree, I thought to myself, I sure wish I had a pair of Richard's pants on right now since I was straddled on a limb right above him.

I had been keenly aware that Darren had his eyes on Maggie from Goshen Mennonite Mission Church (the pastor's daughter). They were always hanging out together at the youth meetings, but that did not make me like him any less. Darren was a nice-looking guy—two and a half years older than me. He was kind-hearted, funny, and always wanting to lend a hand. He had many other attributes that made him likeable, but with Darren coming to my rescue, I could barely breathe, much less think of all the reasons I liked him so much. As Darren released the branch from my dress, he extended his hand to mine, and as I looked down, our eyes met and we exchanged smiles. If Darren knew how much I cared for him, would he still be my friend? I wondered. Darren turned to face me again smiling, saying, "You are the prettiest little creature that I've ever seen in a tree, but let's get out of this tree and play some softball. Everyone is waiting for us."

Mom let me have the afternoon off from working in the garden, so I hurried alongside him to the field in front of my house. Darren and I had known each other about four years. I would see him almost every day—he was at my house or I was at his—hanging out with Carol. I always enjoyed being in his presence although we never talked much. Carol and Darren were always fighting, and she would tell me how mean he was to her and I was forbidden to be nice to him.

After the softball game I thought about the evening chores, which was probably a good thing. At least when my hands were busy, it did not give me much time to think about things—especially about Darren.

After dinner I helped Mom, Ann Marie and my foster sisters with the dishes and tidied up the kitchen. "Many hands make chores get done much quicker," Mom exclaimed happily. She added, "How about helping me and your siblings snap green beans? I would like to start canning them tonight." My mother at this time was blessed with six children, Richard, Ann Marie, Steve, Keri, Dennis, and me.

I replied, "Of course I will lend a helping hand!"

"So how did you get blood on your dress?" Mom asked suddenly as she stared at the spot on my dress.

"Oh, just scraped my leg a little," I replied with a grin. I dare not tell Mom I was climbing trees. She would probably lecture me about it being unladylike and very dangerous. That night I lay in bed staring at the ceiling, tumbling things over in my mind. I thought about my encounter with Darren and how he picked me first to be on his soft-ball team. He actually let me pitch the entire game. I caught him glancing at me often during the game. We did not talk much during the game, but I didn't mind as I was kind of shy toward him. At the end of the game, in a surprise gesture, Darren touched my chin and turned my head so I was looking directly at him. My chest fluttered with the sensation of his touch, and it was a struggle to keep my balance. I thought I was going to pass out.

"Sharon, you are a good pitcher—you can be on my team anytime!" he said, smiling.

A huge grin spread across my face and blushing, I said, "You mean it, Darren?" "Of course I do," Darren replied while nodding his head.

Darren's parents were not Mennonites but allowed him to attend church services including all youth meetings. Darren accepted Jesus as his personal Savior at age eleven at Montgomery Hill Baptist Church where his parents were members. After moving from Silver Spring to Laytonsville, his parents met the pastor at Goshen Mennonite Church. He built their house and they became friends.

After Darren's father had his second heart attack, his parents started going to the Mennonite church regularly. The pastor fell in love with Darren and knew he had many qualities. Darren was warm-hearted, charming, caring, and silly. His contagious energy and enthusiasm filled many hearts. The pastor would talk to Darren often about joining the Mennonite Church and someday becoming a minister. The pastor's daughter Maggie also saw many good qualities in Darren, and they became very good friends.

Goshen Mennonite Mission Church had youth meetings every Saturday night, usually at the pastor's home. Richard, Ann Marie, and I were often invited to attend Goshen's youth meetings since our home church (Gaithersburg Mennonite Mission Church) did not have youth gatherings. We would play games, sing hymns, and have devotions.

After the meetings Richard would drive Darren, Carol, Ann Marie, and me home.

One night after having a blast with my Mennonite friends, Trisha (she was the president of the youth group) approached me as I was getting into Richard's car. "Sharon," Trisha mumbled, "can I talk with you for a minute?"

I replied, "Of course, what is it?"

She began talking with tear-filled eyes, "Paul (the pastor) does not want you here again nor your brother and sister. He has banned you guys from our youth meetings. He thinks you and Richard are a bad influence on the Goshen youth."

I could not believe what I was hearing—me a bad influence! I was a Christian, Mennonite girl obeying all the rules—no makeup, no swearing, dresses below the knees and wearing my covering at all times. I knew I had a personal relationship with God. I talked to Him many times during the day. Whenever I had time I would witness to my neighborhood friends, inviting them to my church, always telling them how awesome God is. Richard was the kindest, most respectful guy out of all the boys there besides Darren. Ann Marie's best friend attended the youth meetings. Ann Marie always looked forward to Saturday evenings so she and her friend could hang out together. Why is the pastor kicking us out of the youth group? I couldn't tell our parents; they would be so upset and hurt. I thought to myself, what have I done to cause the pastor to think I am a bad influence?

I remember visiting with my neighbor, Mrs. Olson a week ago and she asked me "What is a Christian?"

"A Christian means a person like Jesus Christ," I answered back. I continued to explain to her that being a Christian means having a personal relationship with Jesus Christ and that in order to have that relationship you must ask him to forgive your sins and ask him to come and live inside your heart. I was always sharing my faith with others. I did not want anyone to miss out on Heaven. So why was I such a bad influence? Again, I felt like a small boat lost at sea with no help in sight.

As I was riding home with Richard driving, Darren in the front seat, Carol, Ann Marie, and me in the back seat, I asked them, "What is so bad about Richard and me that would give the minister a reason for banning us from the youth meetings?"

Carol replied, "Trisha said that Maggie is very jealous of you. She is afraid that you are trying to win Darren's heart, and she told her father that she did not think you should be included in the Goshen Mennonite youth group."

As for Richard, I am thinking to myself, the minister's grandson had a crush on Carol, and they thought Richard was interfering with that relationship.

That night I turned the radio dial to WRBS and heard Evangelist Billy Graham talking about God's love and forgiveness. Billy Graham reminded us that God is always with us. He is a loving and forgiving God, and we also should always be God-like. He knows what we are going through, and He loves us more than we could possibly imagine. He continued to say that everybody is not going to like us or be good to us so we need to forgive them and try to understand them. Unable to pull myself away, I listened to the rest of the program. I prayed that night asking God to give me strength to cope with the pastor's decision and, most importantly, to forgive him.

A few weeks went by, and I was still trying not to think about being banned from the Goshen Mennonite youth meetings. Every time I thought about never being able to socialize with my Mennonite friends again, I would break down and cry. I had always been so happy about life, but the last few years I was becoming overwhelmed with sadness due to all my fears as being so different. I remember my grandmother saying often to me when she would visit with us, "Choosing happiness is the way of life." I was blessed with a very happy disposition.

My grandmother would often say, "Sharon, it seems like wherever you go you create smiling faces."

Well, now I was very sad and wanting my life to be over at age fourteen, and I was thinking how I could end my life. But, I remembered my aunt who became very depressed after contracting polio when she was eighteen, and she took an overdose of medicine to end her life, but was not successful. My parents discussed with me and my siblings that, if you take your life, you will not go to Heaven. I did not want to go to Hell.

It was a beautiful summer Saturday. Having God in my life and doing a lot of praying and forgiving, I was almost back to myself again, laughing and having fun with my neighbor friends. The chores were done, and Carol was on her way over to hang out. Mom was weeding in the garden. My younger siblings were taking naps. Dad and Richard were on a job. Carol was knocking at the door so Ann Marie let her in. We were sitting at the kitchen table trying to decide what we wanted to do today.

I noticed the car keys on the table "Hey," I said excitedly, "let's drive the car around the front yard."

I did this occasionally when my parents were watching. Carol and Ann Marie agreed. We were going to take turns. I was first, Carol second, but Ann Marie did not want a turn. Carol insisted that Ann Marie should have a turn. Ann Marie finally got behind the wheel, Carol in the passenger seat. The next thing I saw, the car was flying through the neighbor's fence, speeding through the neighbor's back yard. The car came to a stop just before hitting the above-ground pool.

What happened next was not pleasant. We were scolded by our neighbor and punished by Mom. Our neighbor had to call a tow truck to pull the car out of her backyard. Ann Marie was very emotionally upset and ran sobbing to her bedroom and did not come out for the rest of the day. Carol and I had to pay for all the damages so we cleaned houses for the next several months in order to pay for all the repairs.

Carol never told her parents about the accident. She did not want her dad taking her driving privileges away. On many occasions he would give her the keys to his car and allowed her to drive five miles down the road to the country store for an afternoon snack (Carol was only fourteen years old). I remember one summer afternoon I rode my bike to her house and saw she was bent over picking rocks up from the yard. I asked her if she could ride her bike with me later but she replied back, "I have a better idea, I am going to ask my dad if I can take the car for a ride."

After four hours of picking up rocks out of the yard, he rewarded her with the keys and $2.00.

Carol turned to her dad and said, "May Sharon ride with me?"

He replied back, "If she promises not to talk to you while you are driving."

I answered, "Of course I will not talk to her."

We made it home safely and Carol's dad asked me not to breathe a word about this to anyone, especially my parents.

Chapter 9

EVENING BIRDS' KNOLL

Over the next several weeks I helped Mom every day. I was helping out with my younger siblings, doing house chores, and canning fruits and vegetables. My parents raised a very large garden of vegetables every year. I heard Mom yelling, "Sharon, where are you? Please come get Dennis. He has just messed in his diaper. I'm busy shelling peas, and when you are done changing his diaper, can you please do a load of laundry?"

It seemed as though I was always changing dirty diapers. I had two siblings in diapers, Dennis and Kerri, and they were also a handful—always into something.

Life was not always fair, but I knew there was no point in arguing, so I shouted back, "Okay Mom! I'll do a load of laundry as soon as I change diapers!"

Ann Marie did not have patience with the younger children, so I had the responsibility of keeping them clean, fed, and safe while our mother worked in the garden; sometimes we would not see her for most of the day. Ann Marie was responsible for making sure all the beds were made and the house was swept.

As much as I loved children, they did try my patience. I was always picking up after them and cleaning their dirty finger-prints off the windows and doors. They would drag sand from the sandbox into the house. Sometimes I wished I had been born a boy, just so I could spend more time outside, cutting grass, or baling and bucking hay at the neighbor's farm with some of my neighbor friends, since I loved and worshiped nature and the sun.

Almost every evening after dinner, my siblings and I would help with the outside tasks, sweeping the walkways and driveway and watering plants and the yard if necessary. Mom was very attentive to her garden and flower beds and bushes surrounding our home and yard. She poured so much care into mulching, planting, weeding, transplanting, and watering.

It was after 8:00 p.m., and the sun was setting, yet Dad and Richard still had not returned from work. My father's stone/masonry business was booming; many nights they would work until dark.

Mom, Ann Marie and our foster sisters sat on the side porch, talking about our busy day while my younger brother, Steve played hide and seek with his friends. Watching Steve running and laughing brought tears to my eyes. It was a miracle that he could see. That horrible very dark day of my life, about four years ago, a day I will never forget. Mom had asked Richard to take the trash out after dinner one night. I was in the back yard playing with Steve who was almost three years old at the time. The sun was setting. We were not allowed to burn trash until early evening. Dad was still at work, and Mom was in the kitchen baking cakes.

As Richard was burning the trash, he pulled a plastic bleach bottle out of one of the trash bags and put it aside. He asked me to keep Steve away from the jar lids he had scattered around the fire while he melted the plastic container. As the plastic melted, the jar lids became full. It all happened so quickly; I saw the hot melted plastic flying through the air. Steve had thrown a brick, hitting the jar lids. I heard horrible screams, and I saw Steve was covered with this hot liquid, mostly on his face and eyelids. I was terrified of the sight of his face.

I ran as fast as I could to the house. I was scared to death. I thought we had ruined my brother. For about an hour I hid in my mother's cedar chest in the basement, crying and praying that Steve would not lose his eyesight or possibly die. Mom apparently looked out the kitchen window and saw Steve crawling on the ground screaming. As I was told later, Mom hurried to Steve, picked him up and started running up the road trying to find help. She was definitely scared for his life.

Mom was yelling and screaming, "He's ruined for life! He will never see again!"

A neighbor came to her rescue and drove them to the hospital. The neighbor warned my mother that she did not have brakes but she had a hole in the floor board to stop the car. Mom apparently had no choice but accept her offer to drive them. They made it safely to the hospital in Sandy Spring, Maryland. He was then flown by helicopter to Children's Hospital in Washington, D.C. He had third degree burns on his face and arms. His eyelids were burned severely. After three weeks in the hospital, he was released.

We were told it was a miracle that he did not lose his eyesight. Richard was treated also with second degree burns on his hands. I was nine and Richard thirteen—old enough to know the danger of playing with fire.

"Sharon, what are you thinking about?" Mom asked.

"I answered quietly, "I was thinking about Steve and how lucky we are to have him with us."

"We almost lost him," Mom added. "He had many people praying for his recovery. One of the hardest lessons I've had to learn, Sharon, is that God uses painful circumstances in our lives for good to come out of it."

"What do you mean by that, Mom?" I asked.

Mom replied, "When I was staying with Steve at the hospital I met a couple that had a son who was burned severely over his entire body from a house fire. One day they asked me to pray for their son's recovery. A few days later they approached me and said the doctor informed them that their son would make a full recovery. They thanked me for my prayers and my chats with them about the Lord. They called me a month later and said, "Because of you we are attending church and have God in our lives again."

Mom continued, saying, "Girls, when you have God in your lives He will bring you peace, joy, and happiness."

Just then I heard Steve yell, "Daddy's home!" I saw them walking toward the house, Dad, Richard, and Darren. Darren was helping my dad this summer.

Dad approached Mom and softly speaking, said, "Sure is a beautiful evening like you my dear," as he planted a kiss on her forehead. Dad and Mom always exchanged kisses when saying goodbye or hello.

Darren spoke up smiling, "And it's nice being home!" Darren loved hanging out with my parents. They thought of him as their own son, and they enjoyed his company. He made them laugh at his silliness.

Dad said, "Do you want to know what Darren did to me tonight?"

"Yes we do!" I replied.

"Well, Dad begins, I was using Johnny on the Spot at our job and as I was sitting doing my business, Darren apparently threw a couple of firecrackers at the Johnny on the Spot, scaring the living daylights out of me. I came running out of there with my pants down. I thought someone was shooting at me."

We all laughed so hard–Mom had tears running down her face.

Chapter 10

MYSTIC DANCE PATH

*A*s I combed my hair in front of the dresser mirror, getting ready for the first day of ninth grade, I just wasn't looking forward to another year at a public school. I thought to myself how nice it would be to attend Lancaster Mennonite School in Pennsylvania, a boarding school. My parents informed me that there was no way they could afford the tuition. However, as it turned out, the beginning of my ninth year wasn't so bad. I joined the glee club, and I was taking piano lessons after school. I had a few good friends I enjoyed being with at school.

Ann Marie and I were very blessed to have a wonderful family of sisters, Elizabeth, Betsy, and Tammy, for next door neighbors. They did not see us as being different. They treated us with neighborly kindness and compassion. They often invited us to their home to hang out. One night while hanging out they turned the TV on, and "I Love Lucy" was on. I never laughed so hard in my entire life. I never knew that people could be so funny!

Donna, my church friend (who was in foster care) decided to live with her biological mother again. Donna had been somewhat forced to live as a Mennonite, which she had difficulty doing. She felt like she was in prison with all the Mennonite restrictions. She missed not having a television; she couldn't wear slacks or shorts; she had to wear her hair in two ponytails; and her dresses and skirts had to be worn below the knees. Donna confided in me one day that because her foster mother did not allow her to shave her legs, she wanted to leave. She was so embarrassed about the black hair on her legs. Most Mennonite women do not believe in shaving their legs or underarms.

One of my friends, Barbara, who was in several of my classes said to me one day, "Sharon, did you know Vanessa just got arrested for possession of LSD?"

I asked, "Is that a drug?"

"Yes," Barbara said and added, "haven't you ever noticed her being high?"

I often wondered why she was so strung out but thought she was just having a bad day. I thought to myself, how can anyone do awful things, such as smoking, drinking and using drugs?

I began thinking about the night when the Baltimore/ Washington, D.C. youth group and I were witnessing on the Mall (Washington, D.C.) to crowds of people. I had noticed all the peculiar behaviors and the "hippie" attire and wondered if they were on drugs. I could smell cigarette smoke in the air. The girls had flower garlands in their hair, and some had flower necklaces braided through their hair. Their clothing was free flowing to the ankles, and they wore sandals on their feet. Some of the females seemed very pleasant and were handing out flowers. I was told that the "flower power" is the fad which is part of the "hippie" movement. I approached a young girl holding a bouquet of flowers and told her I would like her to have this tract on "Finding Hope," and she replied, "Will you accept this flower as a token of "peace?"

She then asked me, "Are you part of the Jesus Movement?"

I replied back, "Yes, I have Jesus in my heart and I am here witnessing for Him. Please read the material I have just handed to you and hopefully you will be moved to live a Jesus-like life also."

She then asked me as I was walking away, "Will I need to wear that white thing that you have on your head?"

I answered with a smile, "If you want to obey His Word (the Bible), then yes."

I noticed kids in school this year with band-aid boxes, and I was told they were filled with cigarettes or joints. These classmates, coming mostly from homes of alcoholics and busy parents, had total freedom with their lives. These days I was told were the "far-out days," footloose and fancy free. The kids ran and danced in the streets and stayed out late partying. They were the hard-faced "I dare you to mess with me" kind of kids. I prayed continuously for those kids who had mysterious lives, hoping that they would not end up destroying their lives. I prayed to God to have His angels watch over them. I thought to myself what a scary world, and I never want any part of that kind of life. I wanted to tell them that they only have one life and they are making very bad choices. I thought to myself that I would have my family pray for them that night during our family devotions.

That evening, as usual we came together as a family just before our bedtime to have our evening devotions. I always looked forward to this. We would discuss our day and pray, thanking God for another wonderful day He had given us. My parents always reminded us often to read the Bible daily. Mom would play the piano, and Dad, my siblings and I would sing. We would always sing at least three hymns. My request that night was, "When We All Get to Heaven."

I asked Dad to pray for my classmates who did not know the Lord. That night in bed I cried myself to sleep, thinking that if my parents should die before me how could I live without them. They were my protectors and showed me so much love and I loved them so, so much. The next morning I shared my disturbing thoughts to Mom about losing her and Dad.

Mom nodded and said, "We never know when it is our last day on earth, only the Lord knows, so when it is our time we need to be ready to meet the Lord. Sometimes it is better than living, especially if your body is in pain or sickly." She continued saying, "Heaven is a wonderful place where all of God's people can be together, and there is so much singing and rejoicing all the time. Sharon, there are no bad people in Heaven (I thought to myself, oh how great it would be not to be teased and laughed at); there are no wars and no violence. Do not worry about us dying, Sharon, because God has a special place for us in Heaven, and someday you will come and be with us."

She talked on and on about her God-fearing faith. Her faith was so real that she painted a picture of Heaven in my mind. Her strong faith formed the rock-solid foundation of my faith in the Lord.

My mother, unlike my father, was not raised in a Mennonite home. Her parents belonged to a Lutheran church. My mother, up until she was ten years old, remembers living a very worldly life. They believed in Santa Claus, and they had all the Christmas decorations in their home. She remembers her dad smoking a cigar or pipe every evening in his favorite chair. Mom was raised on a turkey farm in Harrisonburg, Virginia, and one day her father mentioned that he was approached by a Mennonite man asking if he would be interested in selling an acre or two. The Mennonite man said that their church was growing, and they needed to build a bigger church. My grandparents agreed to sell their land to the Mennonites, and two years later my mom, her sisters, and parents joined the Mennonite church.

Chapter 11

SPRING MORNING RUN

Spring had sprung and it was a beautiful spring morning when my parents and I set off from our home in Maryland for Lancaster, Pennsylvania, where I was going to attend school in the fall. I was fifteen years old and was going into the eleventh grade in September. Lancaster Mennonite High School (LMHS) was a private dormitory/school for Mennonite children only.

As the hillsides rolled by, resplendent with fresh green blossoms, I felt a creeping uneasiness. The closer we were getting to LMHS, the more I tried to prolong the trip asking Dad if we could do some sightseeing. We drove down countryside roads and passed many Amish farms. The countryside was so breathlessly beautiful. We saw Amish women hanging their laundry on the front porch of their homes. The men were in the fields, plowing the soil with horses pulling the plows. Children were playing in their yards.

We passed a one room schoolhouse, and I asked my dad to stop. We got out of the car and walked up to the schoolhouse. As we approached the door, we saw it was open. We looked inside and there was only one teacher (about seventeen years old) in the room. The children inside were maybe six to nine years old. The teacher was telling a story from the Bible. It was recess for the older children (age ten to fourteen). They were playing a game of softball outside. They had no shoes on. As I watched, I was very intrigued with the strength of the young boys and how fast they could run around the bases.

The teacher soon came outside and asked, "Why are you here?"

Dad replied, "My daughter loves softball and wanted to watch the girls play ball with the boys."

The teacher smiled and said, "Would you like to join in on the game?"

"No, but thanks for the offer; we are on our way to Lancaster Mennonite High School," I added.

Dad and Mom came to my rescue several months back when they noticed many changes in my actions. A relentless series of friendship losses in the past two years, especially being disconnected with my Mennonite friends after the pastor banned me from attending the church socials, was very hard on me because of my sensitive and loving nature. By the time I was fourteen, I was immersed in what I could only call depression. For nearly a year I rarely smiled. I was just going through the motions of living. My trademark sparkle dimmed tremendously. I was very snappy to my siblings, and I had no patience. I was going to my bedroom after all my chores were done, which included washing the dinner dishes and tidying up the entire house. When I retired for the day, I would be exhausted, but I still had my homework to do. I could not do my homework until after all my chores were done. Usually by 10:30 p.m. I would fall asleep, crying into my pillow.

It was brutal most days at school. I was near the end of the tenth grade, which was the toughest year of all; the first year of high school. The friends I had in ninth grade did not want to be friends with me in high school. They seemed very snobbish; actually they would pass me in the halls and not even wave or say hi. I was pretty much alone. During lunch hour, I would sit in a classroom eating my lunch, or I would go without lunch and read or do my homework.

My parents knew something was bothering me when I would come out of my bedroom only to eat, clean house, and maybe once in awhile go outside to shoot basketballs alone. I pretty much did everything alone. I wanted my life to be over. I was tired of kids staring at me as if I had some kind of a plague. Some kids felt sorry for me; they had pity on me, which bothered me tremendously.

The girl Sherry, who was in my second-grade class, (the girl who accused me of being a copycat about her birthday) sat beside me in biology class. What a coincidence that she was assigned a seat next to me. She never had much to say to me other than "Hi."

I wanted to die, but I did have one friend—it was my Jesus who was my inspiration to want to live. I would talk to Him every day, sometimes three or four times a day. As I knelt beside my bed and prayed, "Rock of ages cleft for me, let me hide myself in thee, so helpless is my heart—all overwhelmed, it looks to you for strength, long it has struggled on and now is crushed again. Please, Lord, give me strength to meet each day. Give me grace to endure the teasing kids at school. Help me to be a better sister. I know I've been very unbearable to live with. In Jesus' name, Amen."

As I got up from the floor with tears filling up my eyes, both Mom and Dad were standing in my doorway with tears in their eyes.

Dad said, "Sharon, may we come in? We need to talk with you."

My reply was, "Of course, please sit down." I sat down on the bed beside them.

Dad began talking first and asked me if I would be interested in going away to a private Mennonite school for the rest of my high school years. I jumped up with tears in my eyes and hugged them both.

"Yes!" I shouted.

I thought it would be so nice to have Mennonite girls in school with me.

"But Dad," I added, "how can you afford to send me away? I know you will have to do without to send me to a private school."

Mom and Dad both agreed they were going to have to make sacrifices, but they wanted me to be happy again. My light had burned out, and they wanted my light to shine again.

As I was beginning to doze off, Mom whispered quietly, "Sharon wake up, we're here." When I opened my eyes I saw so many kids like me. The girls had on skirts to the knees, long ponytails with a covering sitting on top of their heads. The boys, of course, dressed like the worldly boys but were different. They actually smiled at me and asked me if I was planning on attending school there. After my registration was completed, we walked around the school grounds. I was getting really excited about being with young teenagers like me. I would never have to worry about being different, which was so comforting to me. The kids I met today had something very special about their temperament—goodness and gentleness. Driving home after our tour of the school, I thanked my parents for this special day, our spring morning run to Lancaster, Pennsylvania.

Chapter 12

GARDEN SPOT PLACE

The summer passed by so quickly. I arrived at LMHS a few days before classes were to start very excited, a little scared, but mostly anxious. "What is LMHS?" a lot of my friends in Maryland would ask me. I would tell them, "It is a private Mennonite school where only the Mennonites attend. It is a quaint, peaceful little religious school located in Lancaster, Pennsylvania, where the Amish live (the Garden Spot of the world) which annually helps to entice millions of dollars worth of tourists' money."

There were so many happy faces. Half of us juniors were new at LMHS that year, and at the first social we became acquainted with each other. I met so many wonderful kids. Most of them lived at home with their parents, near the school, and commuted by bus or car every day. Some came as far as thirty-five miles from school.

Looking across the room, I noticed many different styles of clothing. The boys wore blue jeans, bibbed overalls, or flared slacks. The girls were wearing maxi or midi skirts with sandals, which are accepted by the world, since at this time (the early '70s) the fad was the "hippie" attire. Most of the girls wore their hair in two ponytails with a covering on top of the head. There were a few very plainly dressed Mennonite girls (cape dresses and hair up in a bun with a large covering on). Every face looked so happy, including mine, I'm sure. There were shrieks of laughter coming from many groups of conversations going on.

As Mary (my home church friend) and I approached a group, a couple of girls broke away from their circle and introduced themselves to us. The first girl, Leanne, very pretty, asked us if we were new and if we would like to join them. We thanked her and agreed we would love to.

One of the girls said, "Do you know this is the first year we do not have to wear our hair up in a bun, and the cape dress is not mandatory?"

"Really?" someone replied. "That is wonderful news."

The Mennonite rules about capes and coverings were strictly enforced at the school prior to this year.

"Apparently the students had been fuming for a couple of years about doing away with some of the restrictions," one of the girls in our group added to the conversation.

Our first social was a hayride to a farm a few miles from the school. As Mary and I piled into an already crowded wagon, we were soon on our way, singing, laughing, and telling jokes. Wow, so many smiling faces. I turned to my friend and roommate, Mary, whispering, "We are going to have fun this year!" Mary nodded, agreeing with me.

At the farm we divided into groups since there were different activities planned for us. We bobbed for apples; we played musical chairs, and we had relay races until it was time for devotions around the bonfire. The fire was the biggest fire I had ever seen; it seemed to light up the whole sky. The night was so awesome, smelling the aroma of hot chocolate and roasting marshmallows. We sang and listened to a short scripture reading from the Bible and then were led in prayer by the president of LMHS.

On our trip back to the school, our wagon had the best-looking guys, it seemed. The boys were so much fun to tease; they were so reserved, unlike us girls. We asked them to take off their sweaters or jackets and share with a girl on the wagon since it was getting a bit chilly. The boy whose jacket I had draped over my shoulders was very shy. He had beautiful dreamy blue eyes. I was told by one of his friends that he was very attracted to me, and he wanted to ask me out but was too shy. He moved closer to me reaching his hand out for mine saying, "You're Sharon?"

"Yes," I said, smiling at him. "What is your name?" I asked.

"Josh," he answered.

As we made small talk, he put his arm around me bringing me closer to him to keep us warm. I wanted everyone to like me, and if conforming to peer pressure was the way for this to happen, I'd allow myself to be pressured from time to time. I was a fun-loving girl who had an adventurous spirit and would hang out mostly with the more worldly Mennonites.

Mary and I shared a room in the dormitory. There were two beds in every room. Emily, another friend we met also stayed in the dorm. Her room was across the hall from us.

It was absolutely necessary to be obedient to the matron of the dorm. She patrolled the halls, and she he had eyes like a cat. During study hours, we could go to other friends' rooms only with permission from the matron. And, of course, after lights out (ten o'clock) we were all supposed to be in our beds.

On the first day of school, the bell rang to wake us up. We got dressed and hurried to the cafeteria which was in the basement of the auditorium. There were six chairs to a table, and we were not excused from the table until everyone had completed their breakfast. The scrambled eggs were the best I ever had.

Most of my teachers were dressed very plain. I had six classes, which were English, Mathematics, Earth Science, Physical Education, World Culture, and Typing II/Public Speaking. Life at LMHS was fascinating to me. I believed in myself again. The last four years I thought I was so boring and that no one wanted to be my friend. I was now happy once again, and I was very entertaining to all my new friends. There was never a dull moment with my new group of friends. Most of the girls in my group commuted to school every day.

After lights out one night, Mary and I climbed out of our dorm window and met up with other friends at the Lancaster drive-in theater about a block from our dormitory. Josh, the boy that had a crush on me was also at the drive-In with his car. Josh commuted to school every day. Mary's guy friend, Bruce, had his hot rod at the drive-in also. I jumped in Josh's hot rod. Most every wild Mennonite boy owned a hot rod, including my brother Richard. Richard owned 1972 orange Road Runner. I was so impressed with my brother always winning the car races he and his friends had on the weekends.

I had never been to a movie in my life. It was awesome. A waiter came to the window and took our order. I don't remember much of the movie. I think it was *The Sting.* Josh and I talked about our families and our plans for the future.

One night Mary never returned to the dorm. The matron of the dormitory, Ruth, was very angry with me because I did not report it to her. I found out the next day that Mary was dismissed from the school. Her parents were called and told to come for her immediately. I remember Mary would never open her books in study hall or in our room. She always, though, managed to score very high on all her assignments. I thought the girl was the most brilliant kid I had ever known. I thought often to myself that Mary, someday, would be very successful.

My friends and I continued sneaking out after lights out; it was all good. There was no sex, no drinking, no smoking; just a lot of joking around and playing pranks on each other. One evening after study hall, Emily and I decided to meet up with our guy friends. We climbed out of our bedroom window and walked to the drive-in to catch the ending of *The Exorcist.* As we watched the ending, Josh pulled me close to him, kissing my head and whispered to me that he would like me to be his girlfriend. He put his hands on my chest and started rubbing my breasts. My heart started beating fast and faster. This was all new to me. Actually, I could feel my blood pounding through my body. I was having the same sensation as when I heard my parents making love.

Josh was staring down at me trying to get a reaction or answer from me. I was thinking to myself, I wish I had my pillow! Or maybe

I should ask him if he would like to hump me. I raised my eyes to meet his and softly replied that I would have to think about it. A deep sense of longing inched its way into my soul as I continued staring at Josh. My thoughts then turned to Darren, who made me promise him that I would not get serious with anyone. Darren was very special to me, and I was already looking forward to our upcoming summer together again.

The year at LMHS was coming to an end, and I knew that I had disappointed my teachers and also my parents. I was at LMHS totally for the social events. I had no intentions of studying for quizzes or tests. I was too busy being the social butterfly. I played field hockey and basketball for LMHS and sang in the LMHS choir. Other than that, I pretty much did what I wanted. As I prepared for bed one night, I heard something hit my window. I opened the window and looked down and saw Josh and his friend smiling up at me, asking me if they could come in to visit. I told them to meet me at the back door. Somehow we made it back to my room without the matron seeing us. We sat in the room and just talked.

Josh turned to me and said, "Guess what, Sharon, you are not going to believe this; we are cousins, but distant."

I jumped up and said, "You are kidding me!"

"No, your great grandmother and my great grandmother are sisters," he replied.

I was in disbelief. I knew now that we could no longer be interested in each other as boyfriend and girlfriend. We continued talking about being related and played scrabble until we heard a knock at the door. I told Josh and his friend to get under the bed. It was too late. The matron opened the door and was furious with me for having the guys in my room. I was given one week to find another home, so I could finish the year out (one month to go). My friend, Katie who lived near Lancaster, offered me a place to stay with her brother, who had a large farmhouse.

My parents were very disappointed in me when they received a call from the school principal that I was asked to leave the dormitory for the remainder of my school year. They informed me that I should not bother coming home on the weekends since I had only a few weeks of school left. Usually I would go home every weekend since there were a few kids from the Washington DC area attending LMHS, so I had a ride home.

After moving in with Katie's brother and his wife Linda, my girlfriends and I would hang out from Friday night until Sunday night. I had only three weekends left before school was over for the summer. The first Saturday morning living on a farm, I was awakened by the sound of a rooster crowing in the barnyard. Opening my eyes to a bright sun-filled room, I jumped up and stretched and looked out the window. I saw a horse and buggy coming up the lane. As I stared out the window taking in the awesome countryside, I heard a soft knock at my bedroom door.

"Good morning Sharon, it is time that you get up and enjoy the day!" said Linda cheerfully. I opened the door and there she stood, Katie's sister-in-law, Linda. Linda (six years older than me) was really cool, I thought. She would get up at 4:00 a.m. to help her husband milk the cows and do all the daily chores. Their day was over at 7:00 p.m., and they would retire to the bedroom by 8:30 p.m. every night.

"Hey Sharon, the reason I am here is that I was wondering if you could please give me a hand in the barn, milking the cows. Len is busy working in the fields with a few Amish neighbors."

"I would love to help you," I answered as I slipped out of my nightgown and put on a pair of trousers that Linda had tossed at me. I had never had trousers on before and as I zipped them up, I noticed Linda with a big grin on her face saying, "Sharon, you don't look bad in pants" and I gave her a nod thanking her for the compliment.

I did notice she would wear pants only when she was working in the fields or milking. When she was not working alongside of her husband, she wore maxi skirts and a ponytail with her covering sitting on top of her head. I thought they were a very warm and easygoing couple. I felt comfortable talking to them about anything. They would encourage me to entertain my friends in their formal living room. They did not give me a curfew when to be home. I did pretty much as I pleased.

I hurried to the barn with Linda leading the way. I watched her milk a few cows, and then she handed me the milking unit. Thankfully, she had given me trousers to put on! The morning went by pretty fast. Actually I loved everything about the farm life, except for the smell of the manure. Linda turned to me and said "Sharon, I noticed you were daydreaming; are you in love?"

I chuckled, "No, but I am having a blast with my friends," I replied.

"Do you want to share with me what you did last night?" she asked.

I gave her a nod and shared with her my first experience at the "barn" which was located in Lancaster, about twenty minutes by car from where I was staying. Every Friday night the Mennonite youth in the Lancaster County area would hang out and play games, chit chat, and meet new Mennonite friends. They would have contests, such as the best singing group, the best talent shows, or the best comedian. I referred to this gathering as a "meet market." I began saying "Leanne invited me to go with her and Emily to the "barn." We could not get a ride so Leanne suggested we should just start walking. After twenty minutes of walking, they dared me to put my thumb out. I was hitch-hiking, they told me. I pulled my hand back to my side, but it was too late, a pickup truck pulled over. Leanne apparently recognized the young man and he yelled at us, "You are foolish to be hitch-hiking at this time of day!" It was beginning to get dark, so we jumped in the back of the pickup truck and off we went down the road."

"At the "barn" we met a few guys there. We left the "barn" catching a ride to the Blue Ball Fire Department where they have Friday night dancing. They were country square dancing, so we joined in along with the Mennonite guys we had just met at the "barn." Mark was my partner. "We closed the dance hall down. Leaving the Fire Hall, we decided to go into Lancaster to ride around the "loop." We had so much fun waving and shouting at bystanders. I had the best Friday evening ever, and I am feeling so lucky to have found such wonderful friends that I can have fun with."

Linda thanked me for sharing my story with her and thanked me for giving her a hand with milking as we walked back to the house for lunch. Later that day, I received a phone call from Leanne asking me if I would walk over to her house, that she had a surprise for me. When I arrived an hour later, she was making dinner.

I asked, "What is the surprise"?

She grinned, "You have a new boyfriend and I have a new boy-friend, and we are going to serve them dinner tonight." Leanne's parents were out of town and she was babysitting her younger brothers. A car pulled into the driveway. I noticed the car and the guys from the night before. I was wondering which guy liked me. The tall, broad-chested guy, with sandy blond hair walked toward me and bent down and gave me a kiss on the tip of my nose. Thank God it was Mark who liked me because it would be awkward to have a boyfriend whose name was the same as my brother.

Mark grabbed my hands and walked me to the mirror in the foyer hallway. I could see our reflection in the mirror. Mark was very handsome and said, smiling, "Are we not going to make an awesome couple?"

I agreed, saying, "Okay, do you remember my name?"

"Of course, it is Sharonia from Washingtonia, D.C." He continued saying, "Don't you miss your folks back at home?"

"Yes, but my parents are really displeased with me for not obeying the dormitory rules and being kicked out. Also my mother just gave birth to a baby a month and a half ago and is very busy with my baby sister," I replied.

After dinner we started a bonfire and had our dessert, funny cake pie and a scoop of homemade vanilla ice cream that Leanne's brothers had made earlier. Mark and Steve both agreed they enjoyed the evening and thanked us for the fabulous fried chicken dinner. They invited us to go roller skating in Lancaster the next Friday evening. We both nodded our heads affirmatively. In the glow of the moonlight, we waved goodbye to our new guy friends as they backed out of the driveway.

Friday evening did not come soon enough for me. I was so looking forward seeing Mark again. He was a couple years older than me, having graduated from Lancaster Mennonite school the previous year and was employed with his father, building log cabin houses. Leanne, Katie and I visited the roller rink a couple of times due to me begging them to take me so I could practice before Friday night's date. I had never roller skated before; what a hilarious sight the first night. I was on my butt more than I was on my feet. Leanne and Katie were fabulous skaters. They skated with so much elegance. I was knocking people over and running into the walls and then bouncing off and flying through the air. The next morning, I could not get out of bed. I ached from head to toe. I was lucky I did not hurt someone or myself. I often heard if you can ice skate, you will not have a problem roller skating; that is a bunch of malarkey!

On Friday night Mark picked me up in his pickup truck, and Steve and Leanne were following us in Steve's car. Mark and I were hand-in-hand most of the night, unless he wanted to show off some of his fabulous stunts. He could skate in little circles, backwards and sideways. He was the best skater there, I thought. At the last round of skating for the night, Mark skated behind me and rested his hands on my hips and guided me around the rink with us both synchronized with each other's skating, left, right, left, right. Then all of a sudden he tried lifting me but both of us went crashing to the floor. I landed on top of him, crushing him, I am sure, but he jumped up and grabbed me around the waist, lifted me up and gazing in my eyes, apologized. He held me firmly in place until I was able to get my balance again on my skates.

He kissed me very gently on the forehead and grabbed my hand, guiding me to the bench. He breathed into my ear whispering, "Sharon, I love your body. I hope I didn't hurt it in any way when you fell."

On our way home, he offered to stop for ice cream but I told him I had dessert waiting for him back home.

He winked and asked, "Oh yeah, is it the funny cake pies?"

"No," I said grinning, "It is Sharon's whoopie pie." We laughed.

After we had dessert, I invited him into the formal living room. I turned on some soft music and sat down next to him. Mark leaned over to kiss me but paused and asked if he could kiss me. I raised my lips to his, and we kissed passionately for hours it seemed. I didn't want to stop kissing him, knowing that I might never kiss him again since I had only one more weekend in Pennsylvania. "Oh no!" I shouted as I jumped up gazing down at Mark and softly added, "Mark, you need to leave. Can you believe it is almost 4:00 a.m.? Linda and Len will be getting up soon." We had fallen asleep in each other's arms. I followed him to the door and said goodnight.

After another long week of school, I was looking forward to spending time with Mark. Katie's parents were out of town, and Katie's brother (he was eight years older than Katie) had the responsibility of keeping an eye on her. Katie's boyfriend's best friend played in a band so Katie begged Len to allow her to have a party at the house. He agreed and said only if he and Linda could chaperone.

We decided to have the party in the field behind Katie's parents' house. It was a warm May afternoon. We began a game of volleyball and played until dusk. Then we started a bonfire and listened to the band. The band was playing the top forty songs. What awesome melody and harmony. They were surely gifted with fabulous voices. There was no drinking, dancing, smoking (cigarettes or joints), just a lot of food and soft drinks.

Mark arrived with a few other friends. By 9:00 p.m. we had a big crowd of about fifty Mennonites from age seventeen to about twenty-one. We sang and swayed to the music. The night flew by, and Linda and Len retired to their bedroom. We promised them that we were not going to do anything that would harm any of us.

A few of my friends persuaded our guy friends to spend the night. Mark and I flopped onto one of the mattresses on the floor. Mark took his shoes off and then mine. I looked up and saw Mark's friend coming toward us with a big pizza. "No thanks" I said and Mark said, "If I eat anything else, except for Sharon, I will upchuck all over this place."

I gazed into his eyes and laughingly said, "Are you thinking about eating me?" I was thinking about the oral sex garbage I saw in that book several years ago when I was babysitting my neighbor's children. Mark leaned over me and started laughing uncontrollably, "No, Sharon, but I am going to sleep with you." Of course being raised Mennonites, we were taught that having sex before marriage meant you would definitely go to hell. There was no discussion about it; we did not talk about or act upon it. It was embedded in our minds that you save your virginity for your wife or husband.

After all the lights were out, Mark grabbed my hand and squeezed it gently. He hardly touched me and I could feel the blood pounding through my body.

I whispered in his ear, "Have you ever dry humped a girl?" and he replied back, "No, I only have humped over a girl before playing leap frog; and I think she was a horny frog and I was a horny bull frog."

I laughed so hard that everyone wanted to know what I was laughing about so I told them, and we all laughed together.

I jumped up and turned on the lights saying, "Let's play leaping the horny frogs." We had so much fun playing that we forgot about how horny we were a few minutes ago.

Sunday came too soon. We were awakened by Linda and Len shouting at us, "Time to get up; we are all going to church!" Linda announced that the pancakes were in the oven staying warm for our hungry bellies.

We did work up an appetite after playing leap frog. Mark and I and I'm sure that the others experimented with the dry humping also, since I did hear a few moans. Mark and I climaxed several times during the night as we dry humped with all our clothes on, of course. We enjoyed making each other laugh. I shared with him the experience when I was twelve years old, and my neighbor guy friend threw me on the ground and started humping me and I was terrified but remembered it felt awesome. I couldn't bring myself to share my addiction of pillow humping though; I was so ashamed of myself for even doing something as ridiculous as that.

Monday morning came too soon, but I was up and dressed within minutes and waiting for the bus to pick me up, along with Leanne and Katie. The ride to school always seemed more than an hour long, especially if we got caught behind a horse and buggy.

Today I wanted to sit alone and just think about my year spent in Pennsylvania. I knew I was going to miss all my friends. I mostly would miss all my friends that I became so close to. We did every-thing together and spent every possible moment with each other. We lived every day to its fullest. We fought for our individuality; we were all so different but I felt we had so much in common, maybe because we were of the same faith, Mennonite. We expressed our feelings. We laughed together. We would talk about our future. We found unity in diversity. We grew through are relationships. We struggled in our World Culture class together. I felt as if I were saying goodbye to my family.

I even became friends with some of my teachers. Actually, they were giving me encouragement to allow Christ to be the center of my daily activities so I would find life worth living. I thought to myself, for the first time in many years (since I started middle school) that I finally felt life was awesome and so enjoyable. When one of my teachers heard I was kicked out of the dormitory, she informed me that I need to make wiser choices and select wiser friends. Stay away from the fools because you will end up with a very unfulfilling life. Proverbs 15:14 (NIV) says, "A wise person is hungry for knowledge, while the fools feed on trash," and she continued to advise me to give my life completely to the Lord and serve Him wholeheartedly. I knew in my heart that I was not living the straight and narrow. I had made many mistakes that past year, but they were lessons learned. I just wanted to have fun and be accepted for me, and I accomplished that. I wanted to have many, many friends. I wanted to have a blast in school.

For the first time since seventh grade, I really enjoyed getting up every morning and going to school. We played pranks on each other between classes. I always looked forward to lunchtime because I did not worry about eating alone. I had friends begging me to eat with them. The last week of my junior year at LMHS flew by. On Thursday evening Mark stopped by to say goodbye. I heard his strong knock, ran to the door and opened it to find a beautiful smile on his face.

"Sharon, he said gently, it is so good to see you but I cannot say goodbye tonight or ever. You are my sunshine! You are my everything! I have so much fun with you, and I can't bear to think about you leaving tomorrow. Something in your smile makes me feel things I've never felt before. I'm feeling love for the first time. Being with you, looking into your eyes, holding your hand, touching your cheeks, makes me feel that love was made just for us."

He was grinning and said, "Sharon, I want to do something special tomorrow before you leave for home."

I replied, "Well, my dad is picking me up right after my last class, which is about 3:00 p.m."

His eyes glowed with excitement, "I want to have lunch with you tomorrow. I will pack our lunch and we will walk to the stream behind the school and there we will say our goodbyes at the last possible minute."

I agreed that it would be a date.

Mark stayed a few hours, and we played scrabble and listened to Neil Diamond, who was my favorite artist. Mark jumped up and took my hand and led me to the sofa where we snuggled with each other until it was time to say goodnight.

It was the last day of school. I had never shed so many tears, saying goodbye to all my friends and teachers. I met Mark at the stream at lunchtime to say goodbye to him. He promised me he would stay in touch and was hoping I would welcome that. He grabbed me and pulled me to his chest and whispered that he was going to miss my beautiful smile and my fun-loving spirit. "Sharon," he asked, "do you think it will be possible you could come back this summer to visit?"

Again, In the back of my mind, I was thinking about spending my summer with Darren. I promised Darren that I would not get serious with anyone but just have fun with the guys. The bell chimed, indicating lunchtime was over. Mark and I stared at each other in admiration, not touching but smiling at each other, and he was the first to speak.

"Sharon, I am not good at saying goodbye, so I am not, but promise me that you will never forget me," he murmured in my ear.

I promised I would stay in touch.

Chapter 13

MOONLIGHTING PATH

When Darren and I began to hang out after the end of my junior year at LMHS, I was so happy that we were together again. We did everything together. We spent every minute possible together. Darren and I had been friends for many years, but we never seemed to connect in the romance department until now. We spent many nights under the moonlit sky, watching the stars and just chatting about our days. One night we decided to lie under the stars by the flowing stream behind my house.

Darren gave me a loving gaze, saying, "Sharon, I want to grow old loving you. I can't imagine you not in my life. You are my hope and joy. There is nothing I would rather do than live my life in love with you. You bring so much fun to our relationship. We have so many happy memories and all the little kisses and hugs here and there. I don't think I can exist without you." I smiled and gave him the most passionate kiss ever. My tongue was exploring every inch in his mouth.

Darren and I would play a lot of board games with my younger siblings when my parents were attending Amway meetings or having meetings at the house. Mom was a great saleswoman; she could sell anything. I think it was because people really liked her.

She was so genuinely nice and very likable. My parents became direct distributors with Amway in record breaking time.

One night, Darren came over to hang out. He said, "Sharon, let's go for a ride."

I got into his car and sat next to the passenger door. He reached over and pulled me next to him as we were leaving my driveway. Darren drove maybe about a mile and he pulled over. He turned off the car. He wrapped his arms around me. He held me in his arms and his head went back against the seat and he murmured, "Sharon I want you so, so bad!"

He was now staring into my eyes and for the first time in my life, I wanted him to kiss me so badly. I was feeling very warm all over. I was melting in his arms. I wanted to feel his tongue in my mouth again. We kissed and held each other for hours. He ran his fingers down my cheeks and planted a warm kiss on my ear lobe whispering, "Sharon, I miss you so much when I am away, and I am not looking forward to leaving you again."

I said, "Darren, do not worry about us. We have the rest of our lives to spend with each other. We must think only right now about getting our education and someday, you'll be the best minister, and I will be by your side."

He and I would often talk about how many children we wanted and discussed the names for them. Darren was my best friend and soul mate. I never really thought much about Mark again after spending time with Darren.

As the summer was coming to an end, Darren stopped in to see me one night. We decided to sit in the living room since my parents had already gone to bed. We were talking about our future together. He wanted to know if I planned on going to Eastern Mennonite College in Harrisonburg, Virginia after my senior year. I told him that my parents were very upset with me about my grades. They stressed to me that if I did not do better in my senior year, I would probably be attending the Community College.

My mind drifted back to the last day of school when my dad and I were discussing my grades on our ride home from Lancaster. He told me I possibly might not be returning to LMHS for my senior year. He was very disturbed about my grade average and said that he is not going to spend money that he didn't have because I was not interested in doing my best. Dad quoted me a scripture from the Bible, "It is senseless to pay tuition to educate, while the fool feeds on trash."

Darren said, "Listen to me Sharon, if you do go to Eastern Mennonite College in Harrisonburg, I will transfer so I can be with you, okay? I can't stand the thought of you down in Virginia and me in Pennsylvania." He brought me closer to him, and I cuddled up against him, with his arms holding me so tight. I was thinking to myself maybe we should go to the basement before we get caught. My parents even had a hard time accepting us just holding hands. I wanted Darren to kiss me again like the night when we were parking.

Darren opened his heart to me saying, "I just want to hold you in my arms forever. I want to hold you tight against me. I enjoy staring into your eyes and seeing the peaceful look on your beautiful face. When I am with you, I'm in Heaven. Being separated from you is really tough. It is like this is some sort of test or trial that I must go through. I do know one thing; it certainly makes me appreciate and cherish the time that I do get to spend with you!"

I kissed him gently on the cheek and murmured in his ear, "Darren, I will forever love and cherish you. For in you is my hope, my joy and peace."

I didn't want this night to ever end, but my father surprised us by turning the light on. He startled us as he blurted out, "What are you guys doing? You need to stop that immediately!"

Darren jumped up and said, "Adam I am so sorry, but I was just saying goodbye."

"Bye," I said, and Darren was gone.

Summer of '72 was over too soon. Darren left for college. I would stay in touch writing lots of letters. Each one filled with my love for him and my passion to be with him. I missed his presence and being romanced by his love for me. It was a tough day again;

it had been almost a month since Darren had left and I was feeling really down so I decided to write a note to him.

Hi, Love! Are you enjoying yourself? I hope you're having fun but also behaving yourself at the same time.

Guess what I am doing right now? Wrong, I am watching the Olympics with Carol. I wish you were here by my side watching it with me. Wayne Collect just won the 400 meters. Remember the film we bought? Well, it fits in Carol's camera. Today she took a couple of pictures. Tomorrow evening at 5:30 p.m. we have a football game against Richard Montgomery. I hope we win. Are you practicing very hard for the basketball team?

Darren, I miss you so much, especially in the evenings because I am used to seeing you then. I can't wait until next weekend, that is, if you're still planning on coming home.

This Friday evening we're leaving for Fairfax, Virginia. We are planning to camp, and we plan on visiting the largest pool on the whole Eastern Coast. It's almost a whole acre in size. We are also going to visit a Mennonite church in Virginia and visit with my grandmother in Harrisonburg. Hopefully, God willing, I will be able to walk through the Eastern Mennonite College campus since my grandmother lives a block from the school.

I better soon close this letter. It's not a very long letter, but I'll write again soon. I couldn't find my writing paper, so you'll have to be satisfied with my notebook paper. Darren, I love you!

I hope you like your professors. Well, goodbye for now. I really miss you!

Love always and forever,
Sharon

Chapter 14

FALLING RAIN WAY

After my junior year at Lancaster Mennonite High School, my parents decided to send me back to public school because I was definitely not into my studies at LMHS. I was lucky to maintain a 2.0 average in most of my subjects. I was more interested in having a blast with my Mennonite friends, and I had had no time for books.

The first day of my senior year at a public school was frightening—I wanted to drop out of school. After a month of school, I was reconnecting with a few friends from my freshman year. I joined the field hockey team and met more girls. I began hanging out with them after school. I was still wearing my covering but it was a much smaller covering, and I was wearing two ponytails. I was now more sociable and outgoing. My friend, Carol, Darren's sister, who was dating Richard now, came to my rescue many times when she heard of anyone making fun of my covering.

Darren surprised me by asking me to come up to his school's banquet. I accepted, and his mother (Ms. Margie) offered to drive me to spend a weekend with him. The formal dance was so much fun. Of course, I did not dance because I never danced in my life as it was against my Mennonite beliefs. The Mennonites believed that dancing leads to sex. I did, though, remove my covering from my head and let my long, blonde hair flow loosely around my face. We had so much fun that we stayed up pretty much all night.

The last night together we had a little disagreement. I wanted to break up with Darren after seeing some of the cheerleaders interacting with him. One of the blondes seemed very jealous of me being with him. I noticed they were talking a lot, and I was thinking to myself there is more going on than what he is telling me.

Back at home, after spending the weekend with Darren, I was feeling alone and missed him so much.

I had just received a phone call from one of the pastors of my church informing me the bishop and my uncle would like to meet with me next Tuesday to discuss my standing with the Mennonite Church. I thought I would feel better if I wrote a letter to Darren. I found my notepad and walked outside to our favorite spot by the patio.

Dear Darren,

Guess what? I love you. I miss you so, so much. I've decided to write several letters today. Carol bought another twenty-exposure film today. In two weeks I should have both films developed. I want to keep a couple of those pictures that your mom took of us with her Polaroid camera, and put them in my scrapbook. By the way, thanks for your basketball picture! That's what I call *love* cutting it out of your yearbook! (ha ha).

Mom is planning on taking me shopping tomorrow so I'll try to get a scrapbook. I'll work on it so the next time you come home I'll show it to you.

Darren, I keep thinking about our last night together at your school social. I hope we never have to go through something like that again. It really made me think, though. I was telling myself all day Sunday that it was all over for us, but then I knew I loved you too much to break up. That's what I was thinking about when you asked me what was bothering me.

I didn't want to tell you. I wanted to run anywhere because I was all confused and didn't know if breaking up was the right thing to do, but after I gave your class ring back to you and then when you threw the ring and said, "Sharon you better go and I'll probably never see you again," really hurt me. Darren, I could never leave you just like that. Never, never! I want you so much! I thought it was all over for us, but I wanted so much to be back in your arms. I just wanted to hold you tight and never let you go. Both of us are still young and we have to have some fun yet. I mean that you need to enjoy your social life up there, and I have to do the same. But, just remember, you have a little woman back at home.

I wrote to Emily today, and asked her what weekend I should go up. I'll let you know as soon as I find out. I'd like to visit LMHS when I go to Pennsylvania.

My dad was just talking to me. He said, "You're writing to Darren already—and a long letter at that?"

Darren, please remember me next Tuesday night. Uncle Tom, Pastor Robert, and Bishop Martin are coming to talk to us. I'll write and tell you what the outcome is. Well, I have to soon close this letter; I'm very tired.

Hey, Carol is going to take a picture of me in my bathing suit. Would you like to have it? Nope, you can't have it!

Goodnight lover boy! I love you and I really miss you. I wish you were here tonight to hold me in your arms.

Write soon. I want you to enjoy yourself in whatever you have to do.

Love always,
Sharon

The next Tuesday evening came and only Pastor Robert visited us without my Uncle and the Bishop. He mentioned that the church is very upset with my lifestyle. I was becoming very worldly. He went on to say that unless I asked God for forgiveness, I should not partake in communion this coming Sunday. I told him that I was looking forward to communion, and yes, I planned on taking communion. We prayed together asking God to forgive my worldly ways.

The next evening was Wednesday's prayer meeting which I attended every Wednesday, if possible, with my family. As always my prayer was, "Lord, give me wisdom to be a godly young girl (godly people are those who obey the Word of God). Help me not to gossip like so many of the church members do."

I would often be told or overhear members talking about my mother's lack of discipline with her children. They were blaming my mother for me flapping my wings. After going away to the Mennonite school I did come back changed and different from most of the girls who belonged to my church. I had argued with my parents about not wearing my hair up and not wearing the cape dress ever again.

I do believe there is some virtue in plainness and some truth in those rules, but I wanted to be liked by all people. I did not want to stand out by looking so different. I did know one thing; I did not want to leave God or my church. I still had a vision to become a missionary and serve people. I wanted to help the needy and make a difference in the community. I could feel this dream in my heart and soul.

I was also dreaming about becoming Darren's wife, and having a big family one day. Right in the middle of this craziness, Darren and I had found an oasis of peace, and it was created from the love we have for each other. When I was in Darren's arms, I knew without a doubt that we were stronger than anything life could throw at us. There was magic between us like nothing else I had ever known. I was so grateful every day that Darren was in my life. Knowing that Darren loved me unconditionally kept me going.

I can remember one Sunday evening, after the service, a church friend and I were sitting on the front steps chatting about our upcoming trip to Pennsylvania when I overheard two women talking about how my mother should take parental lessons from my aunt. "Eva Lynn needs to be stricter with her children," I heard someone say.

More and more Mennonites were changing. Some of the rules were getting pushed aside, especially the dress code, but so what. I thought your relationship with God and man was more important than the dress code. Showing love and kindness to everyone was my number one rule. Thinking back several years ago, when I was banned from the Goshen Mennonite youth meeting, I wondered how much gossiping about me aided the decision of banning me from the socials.

Many of the church women were brought into the church by our missionaries. Most of them were unhappily married. Their husbands did not attend church with them, only their children. Most of the children were very unruly and were lacking self-discipline. I think a lot of them were very envious of my family. We were a very happy, kind and loving family.

My mother was a very caring person. She served her community well. She truly loved everyone the way she loved her Lord. I never heard my mother talk badly about anyone, and she was always lending a helping hand. She would often tell me that gossip separates friends. Gossip is the same as murder, and gossip jeopardizes the ministry. People who have sharp tongues often end up cutting their own throats. Gossip can never be taken back. My mother would often say, "No life has ever been made better by gossip and slander. So, let's do what God calls us to do. Let's lay aside all malice and all evil speaking and instead love one another."

Communion Sunday arrived. My mother approached me in the bathroom. "Sharon, I want to talk to you about taking communion today."

"What do you mean, Mom?" I asked.

Mom began speaking, "I was notified by a family member last night that you are still hiking up your skirt at school, and you have been letting your hair down after you get on the school bus. You also just bought a pair of yellow sneakers and I saw a red blouse in your closet. Sharon, you have not changed your worldly ways since our talk with Pastor Robert. You are not being faithful to the church."

"But Mom, I've been thinking about communion and I have prayed to God about the way I've been living; I want to change. I want to be a better Christian, Mom." I cried, "Please Mom, pray with me that I may always do what is right."

I began praying, "Dear Heavenly Father, please give me the wisdom from now on to make the right choices and I am determined to stand on your promise that You are a forgiving God and that you have forgiven me for all my wrong doings. Dear Lord, You know what is in my heart and I want to do what is right; help my weaknesses, dear Lord; I want to live my life in celebration of You. I want to receive everything You have for me, by opening my hands to accept all that you did for me by taking communion today.

Thank You for loving me and setting me free to walk in victory today and always."

I noticed tears in my mother's eyes. We embraced for a long minute. I asked Mom to let the hem out of my dress and she agreed she would. As she pressed my new hemline, we sang "Amazing Grace."

Amazing grace! How sweet the sound, that saved a wretch like me!

I once was lost, but now am found, was blind, but now I see.

'Twas grace that taught my heart to fear, and grace my fears relieved;

How precious did that grace appear, the hour I first believed!

Well, finally it was time to leave for church. I was looking forward to taking communion. I was right with God after asking in prayer earlier that morning for His forgiveness. The Mennonite discipline believes the congregation shall be counseled before communion to learn whether the members are at peace with God and fellowmen and are willing to work in harmony with the discipline of the church. When members absent themselves from communion or are unfaithful to the church, they forfeit their membership. I did not want to absent myself from communion today. I did not want to forfeit my membership. I wanted to be faithful to the church again.

The church believes that open transgressions such as fornication, adultery, lawsuits, drunkenness, dishonesty, and persistent worldly pleasure seeking shall be confessed publicly. I knew that I was not involved with any of those sins.

After Sunday school, I joined the other women upstairs on our side of the church (left side). The men and boys sat on the right side. We sang several hymns. I sat there in awe as the harmony of our voices created beauty. I always enjoyed singing. I was blessed with a beautiful voice, I guess, because I sang solos and duets in the school choir. I always looked forward to Christmas time because I loved singing Christmas carols. Thinking back to my grade school days I would be commended on my singing often by teachers saying I am blessed with a beautiful voice.

My uncle led us in prayer and read the communion scripture. After the sermon, which was given by the bishop, we prepared ourselves for communion in a silent prayer. Communion is observed twice a year. Each believer is given a piece of bread and a sip of grape juice to remember what Jesus did for us. This is only given to those who have given their hearts to Jesus and have been baptized into the church with others who believe as we do.

As all of us were standing, the bishop began passing out the bread, first to the men and then to the women. As he approached me, with my hand extended to receive the bread, he passed me by. I was confused and felt tears filling up my eyes. What does this mean? I thought to myself. Ann Marie was standing next to me with her hand extended to take the bread. The Bishop said to Ann Marie, "This is the body of Christ, broken for you."

The bishop finished passing out the bread and walked toward the communion table to pick up the grape juice. He again served the brethren first, which included my brother. Remember Richard has a bright orange road runner in the church parking lot with the long shoulder length hair to compliment the worldly life. It is amazing that the church advised the boys against wearing neckties but never said anything about the kind of cars they drove or the length of their hair.

The bishop approached me and again passed by me, not saying a word to me. I faintly heard his words to Ann Marie, "This is the blood of Christ, shed for you." Ann Marie sipped from the glass and handed the glass very carefully back to him and then sat down on the pew. I was now the only one left standing. I felt frozen; I could not move; I could not sit down.

When he reached the pulpit, he said in a very stern voice, "Sharon you have not been living a righteous life. Communion is about our fellowship with God. The church feels that you are not right with God so I cannot serve you communion."

I was hurting so badly; my heart felt like a ton of brick. I wanted to cry. I tried to hold back the tears, but I could not. I sat down on the pew and began to sob. I felt someone poking at me. I looked up and it was Jeanette, a very fine Christian, Mennonite lady. Jeanette was fifteen years my senior. She whispered to me, "Sharon, please join us sisters in the basement for feet washing." I obediently followed her to the basement.

Feet washing follows communion. I remember my teacher explaining this ordinance in my instruction class. She said, "We do this because it is a privilege to obey Jesus, and besides, everyone comes with clean feet. The same evening when Jesus used bread and the cup to teach His disciples about His death and suffering for them and all people, He taught them about feet washing. Jesus took water and washed His disciple's feet, and He wants us to wash each other's feet, too. In the Bible days feet got dusty from wearing sandals. Also Jesus wants us to remember how He, the great Son of God, came down to earth to serve people and teach them how to live. He came for all kinds of people, to save all from their sins, by dying for them. We also should be willing to serve anyone.

The women washed feet with women in a quiet place. The men washed feet with men. It is done very quietly; there is no talking.

Another ordinance that is practiced is the Holy Kiss, especially following feet washing. The greeting of the Holy Kiss should be observed and practiced by the believers, brethren among brethren and sisters among sisters, as an expression of godly love. It should be practiced when meeting for worship as well as when meeting for social fellowship. The Bible teaches in I Peter 5:14 "Greet ye one another with a kiss of charity," and in I Thessalonians 5:26 "Greet all brethren with a Holy Kiss." It is holy because it is done with Jesus.

When we reached the basement, Jeanette hugged me and said she would wash my feet if I would wash her feet. I nodded I would. She washed my feet with tears in her eyes, and I was crying and looking for my mom, my aunt, and my cousins. During our feet washing, the deep and reverent silence was broken by an occasional sound of me, Jeanette, and Ann Marie sniffling, fighting back the tears. Ann Marie was sitting next to me waiting to have her feet washed by one of the "Sisters in Christ."

I was informed by Ann Marie that our mother and my aunt were in one of the classrooms. Mom was crying and being comforted by my aunt, I was told. After I washed Jeanette's feet, she embraced me and whispered in my ear, "God loves you and always will." We then exchanged a Holy Kiss. I went to the bathroom to wipe my face and blow my nose. I noticed in the mirror a very sad face. I thought to myself, why me, Lord? I'm a good person; I asked You to forgive me, Lord. Didn't You hear my prayer? How could you allow this to happen, Heavenly Father?

I was so embarrassed. I wanted to run, run far away. I didn't want to go back upstairs for the benediction but I had to go back upstairs to pick up my Bible and purse. As I approached the top step, Richard was standing by the front door waiting for me to come up. He had my Bible and purse in his hand waving them to me. I walked over to him; I noticed he had tears in his eyes, and he was not happy. "Sharon we are leaving now, and we will never be back!" He cried as he opened the door for me.

As we stepped outside, he said, "Take your covering off and leave it here on the door step. They don't want you, either." He meant that our home Church, Gaithersburg Mennonite Mission Church, also had a problem with me.

For the first time since I joined the Mennonite Church, I felt so far from God and all the Bible teachings that were instilled in me. There, looking down on the front steps of my church was my head covering. I always believed a woman wanting to live for Jesus and to follow his teaching would want to cover her head. The covering symbolizes a woman's willingness to obey God's order. It says in I Corinthians 11:5 that a woman who prays or prophesies without a covering on her head does wrong. It even says if she does not wear something on her head, it is as though her head is shaved. This was my understanding since I had taken the instruction classes in order to become a Mennonite.

On the ride home in Richard's bright orange Road Runner, I cried the entire way. Ann Marie was in the back seat, and I could hear her blowing her nose. Suddenly, it got very windy in the car. Ann Marie had rolled down the window and threw her covering out, saying, "God, I am sorry but I don't want to be a Mennonite after the way they just treated my sister."

Richard chimed in and said "Sharon why did you participate in feet washing?"

I mumbled, saying, "Jeanette pleaded with me to join her in the basement, and I did not want to stay upstairs with the men during their feet washing service."

Richard said, "Well, I was very angry about you not being served communion so I stood by the front door waiting for you to come up from the basement." I commented to Richard how caring Jeanette was to me, and I would always remember her hug and Holy Kiss forever and ever and her kind words.

When we approached our house, Richard said to Ann Marie and me, "Change your clothes for bike riding." I put on my culottes which is a skirt but is divided like trousers and cut full to appear as a skirt.

As we were leaving the house about twenty minutes later, the bishop had pulled into the driveway and wanted to talk to me, but Richard politely told him we didn't have time for any discussions.

Throughout the day I would break down and cry. I couldn't help but think about standing up for communion and being denied. Resentment started creeping into my soul; I felt anger, sadness, and rejection. I felt so alone. Now I can't even have a loving and trusting relationship with my own mother and father. I sat along the river bank looking out into the Potomac River and thought about jumping in so I wouldn't have to deal with all these horrible emotions I was feeling. I wanted my life to be over.

Richard walked over to me and said, "Sharon, you are free as that bird now. Look, watch that bird flap his wings. Flap your wings now as you please. Go and live your life to the fullest! You are no longer a Mennonite; there are no more rules!" As Richard was helping me back to my feet from sitting on a big jagged rock by the river, I heard a voice yelling, "Hey, Richard, do you want to ride with us on the bike path?"

I turned my head and saw two African American males with bikes, smiling, "Hey, who is this beautiful girl?" gently spoke one of the guys.

My brother replied, "This is my lovely sister and don't you ever think about hurting her; she has been hurt by too many people but no more."

I thought to myself, I do have Richard; he is my protector and defender and I know he will always be there for me. He was giving me encouragement to start living life again.

PART II

THE UNVEILED DAWN (THE WORLDLY DWELLING)

Chapter 15

EMPTY SONG PLACE

We all have a song, a purpose in life, but I was struggling with who I wanted to be. My life was in chaos. I felt lost, unwanted, and so lonely. I was seventeen years old when my story began as a rebellious teenager.

It was a beautiful Sunday morning. The bedroom windows were opened slightly, just enough to smell the fresh country air under my nose. I heard my younger siblings running down the hallway with their Sunday dress shoes on. I was sure they were getting ready for church. It had been a full week living as a heathen, so my Mennonite relatives would say. As I reached for my housecoat, I heard my mother's voice at my door, "Sharon, I will miss your beautiful voice singing in church today." My mother encouraged me to join every singing group possible. I was told by many people that I had a voice like an angel.

I replied, "Oh Mom, you are so sweet to say that," and I opened the door and we hugged each other.

My mother was hurting so much inside. I know because my mother was a wonderful, loving, caring person, especially to her off-spring. My mother's purpose in life was to live a godly lifestyle and encourage her children and others to be the best possible followers of Christ. It was her desire to see me one day following in her foot-steps, doing mission work. Remember, my parents were missionaries.

When everyone was out of the house, I slowly got dressed. I put on a pair of jeans. I had gone shopping a day earlier and bought my first pair of jeans. I put my long hair in a ponytail, put on sneakers, and walked into the kitchen. Richard was sitting at the table eating toast.

I said, "Good morning Richard, what are we going to do today? It's a beautiful day."

He answered, "Mom and Dad would like us to visit another denomination today and try to find a church that we feel comfortable with." That is what we did. Richard, Ann Marie, and I always did try to obey our parents.

That night I reflected on my first Sabbath day as a non-Mennonite. I was definitely more confused than ever. At the church we visited, the people were so welcoming, reaching out to us with big smiles, embracing us and telling us how happy they were to have us worshipping with them. After the service the pastor and his wife invited us to their home for lunch, but we declined. The congregation was genuinely kind and interested in all the new guests visiting with them. I was having difficulty understanding why my home church thinks I am a sinner and unworthy, and these strangers today think I am a child of God.

I called Darren several times that day but he never returned my phone calls. In my last letter to Darren, I indicated to him that I was worried about our long distance relationship. I had not received a letter or call from him for almost a month. He knew that the pastor and bishop were coming for a visit, but he never inquired about their visit or, for that matter, communion Sunday. I felt that he was deserting me also. I wanted to share with Darren my horrible feelings of being denied communion since he always had a listening ear. I wanted to hear from him that he loves me, which gave me hope for the future.

Well, today was a new day, Monday morning. I was going to make the best of my new day! I was up before dawn and was dressed and out the door before anyone. I was catching a ride with

Carol today; no more school buses. She was waiting for me in the driveway. I had gone shopping a few days before and bought two short skirts with coordinating tops, a new pair of high heels, and a couple pairs of lace panty hose. I really felt good about myself today because I finally might be accepted by the world today! I felt like a million dollars. I jumped in the car as Carol was giving me great compliments on my new outfit. "Sharon, you are going to have all the boys chasing you down the halls today." I just laughed.

As I walked to my first class, I noticed the jocks were looking at me with admiration. After homeroom as I was approaching my first class, a nice-looking boy walked up to me and asked if he could walk me to my next class, and I nodded yes. This attention from the jocks continued for weeks. Carol told me one afternoon, while driving home, that a lot of the senior girls were very jealous of the new "Sharon."

One day as I was approaching the hockey field with my team-mates, a nice looking guy approached me from the sidelines and introduced himself as "Dale" and continued on about how beautiful my teeth were, and he also complimented me on my long, blonde hair. He asked, "May I walk you to all your classes tomorrow?"

I replied, "Sure, but I will have to let Michael know."

I was the happiest girl. I had girlfriends now and boys fighting over me. For once in my life, I finally fit in. Nobody treated me like an outcast or a loser. I felt like my life had meaning, a purpose. I can't help but think about one particular day; the fire drill went off at school and as I hurried out with my classmates, they all wanted me to join their circle of friends. I have never experienced so many worldly friends. I finally felt accepted; I didn't eat lunch alone anymore.

As we were waiting to return to our respective rooms, Dale approached me. "Hi, Sharon," he said, smiling ear to ear, "Can you meet me after school today by the auditorium doors? I want to give you something."

I replied, "My boyfriend is home from college and will be picking me up after school today."

Dale insisted on meeting me so I agreed. He had written a letter asking me to be his girlfriend and, as we were exchanging our goodbyes, he planted a kiss on my cheek. I was so surprised. As I began to walk away I saw Darren waiting by his car. He had seen the kiss! Oh my goodness was he ever furious! Darren was very quiet on our drive home. I began talking as he pulled into my driveway and shared with him my doubts of his love for me since I had not heard from him in over a month. He agreed he was wrong for not calling or writing but asked me to forgive him.

He begged, "Sharon, do not ever stop loving me!" He continued, "Much too often I'm focusing on myself and being the best in basketball and having fun at school and forgetting the most important people in my life, you and God. My purpose is to serve God first and you next! I love life with you! I want to be with you always and forever! I just want you to know, Sharon, I'm always here for you no matter what you decide to do about our relationship."

That night I could not fall asleep due to my breakup with Darren, I am sure. I was so confused but knew this was best for both of us. We both cried as we said our goodbyes. We hugged and kissed each other on the cheek. He said to me as he was walking away, "Sharon, I love you and I hope someday we will be together again. I miss you already. I want to be married to you, and I hope someday you will want that also."

As I was lying awake in bed, many thoughts were running through my mind. I remember telling him he and Jesus shared my heart. Darren was my passion, my dream come true. I think I was being very selfish because I heard he was having a blast with his college friends, and I wanted to have fun also.

My mother cried when I told her that I had broken up with Darren. My mother sadly said, "Sharon, you are making a very big mistake. He is a wonderful Christian and loves the Lord. You both are equally yoked. You are going to be so sorry one day for breaking up with Darren." She loved Darren and thought that he was the perfect guy for me. She also thought he someday would make a wonderful minister. Darren had always wanted to be a minister, and I would tell him I would be the best preacher's wife.

Growing up I dreamed of becoming a missionary someday. I loved people; I enjoyed visiting with families that came to our church services. People were very interesting, and I loved listening to their testimonials and stories. I tried my best, with the Lord's help, to model godliness. I tried to set a good example to the world, but now, I was living like the world. My song for the Lord was empty. Satan had me by the hand, and I was allowing him to live in me. I was going to the homecoming dance with Dale this coming weekend, and I knew I would be dancing and possibly drinking. I have so many worldly friends now, and the only thing that mattered to me was having as much fun as possible. The Mennonites did not want me; they had put me in the world, and I would now be part of the world.

Carol and I went shopping for my dress and I selected a long pink floral, high-waist gown with long, fitted sleeves. That morning I sprayed sun-in on my long hair and sat in the sun for several hours. My blonde hair was one of my best attributes. Dale picked me up in his uncle's Corvette, and away we drove into the sunset to meet up with friends for dinner.

At dinner one of Dale's friends yelled, "Hey, I have a cooler of beer in my trunk, and you guys may help yourself!"

I had never had a beer in my life but I wanted to fit in; I wanted to be accepted. I drank my first beer and did not like the taste; it almost gagged me. Dale had brought with him a bottle of wine so I thought I would try the wine. It went down better. By the time we reached the school to celebrate our homecoming win, I was feeling silly.

The homecoming dance was so much fun. I danced and danced and had the time of my life. I had never experienced so much excitement. At one point, I sat down to take it all in and glanced around the auditorium. I saw so many pretty girls with beautiful updos and gorgeous dresses. I thought to myself, will these girls all have sex tonight with their boyfriends? I saw a lot of kissing and necking going on. The slow dancing, I thought, is why the Mennonites maybe thought dancing could lead to sex.

Chapter 16

STORMY HILL WAY

My parents, especially my mom was very concerned about my new character. She was still trying to protect me from the sinful world. She had found a pack of cigarettes in my purse; I was wearing eye makeup and lipstick which, of course, is against the Mennonite beliefs, and I was wearing immodest clothing. "Sharon," she cried out to me one day as I was leaving for school, "You are ruining your life. For whatsoever one sows that will he also reap. For the one who sows to his own flesh will from the flesh reap corruption. You are headed down a road of destruction, and I can't bear to see you destroy your life."

Richard and I were rebelling, and no one could tell us how to live our lives now. I had always tried to honor my mother and father and obey the Mennonite rules, but I now did not welcome any advice or guidance in my crazy life, living as a heathen. I made the conscious choice to do my own thing now. I wanted excitement: to get high and to have no rules. Richard was also doing as he pleased. He was getting high every day and drag racing whenever the opportunity became available.

As a child, I had learned from the Mennonite Church and my parents that my purpose in life was to know, love, and serve God and the community, and did I love God and people! Of course, all of that changed when I was told I was no longer a follower of God.

I felt God had deserted me; how could He let this happen to me? Anger and resentment took over my life. I began experimenting with marijuana. Richard introduced me to marijuana a few months after we stopped going to the Mennonite Church.

One day, my mother approached me with a baggie of marijuana, and she was crying, "Sharon, is your brother smoking grass?"

Trembling, I replied, "Mom, where did you get this?"

She was now crying uncontrollably and said, "I found it in my bathroom." Richard had taken a shower earlier that day and forgot it, I guessed. Richard enjoyed getting high with his friends since he did not care for beer or liquor.

Springtime was around the corner and things were pretty uncomfortable at home. My father informed us one morning before leaving the house saying, "Hey you all need to start looking for a job because I am no longer going to hand out money to you guys for gas, food, and clothing. You are now on your own."

So after school I applied at Asbury Methodist Retirement Home and was hired. I was hired as a waitress, working Tuesday through Sunday (afternoons only). I really enjoyed the older people; they were so friendly and kind. Many of them became my friends, and I would sit and chat with them after their dinner.

One Sunday, I received a phone call at work. It was my father on the other end crying, "Come home! Something terrible has happened!"

My cousin, Kathleen had passed away. There was a terrible car accident. My Uncle Mahlon, Aunt Maria, and cousins were in a bad car accident. They were on their way to visit a church in Pennsylvania. Kathleen died instantly. Uncle Mahlon and Aunt Maria were rushed to the hospital with life-threatening injuries. Melvin, my favorite male cousin was driving and apparently lost control of the car, and it crossed over into the median and flipped a couple of times. Melvin and Cindy walked away from the accident without any life-threatening injuries.

My father was crying uncontrollably when I arrived home. My dad and mom were getting ready to leave for the hospital and wanted me to watch my younger siblings. Funeral services were held for my cousin Kathleen four days later. My uncle and aunt were not able to attend Kathleen's funeral. The church was packed; people were standing outside trying to hear the service. I approached my cousin Melvin and gave him a big hug and cried with him. The next day my father confided in Richard and me that Uncle Mahlon was not doing well and he would like us to visit him; he had something very important to say to us. We knew it probably had something to do with our rebellious state. We never did get to visit with him because he also succumbed to his injuries.

I saw him a few days later in his casket. My aunt was not able to attend due to her still-serious condition. I cried through the entire service. This was a big loss since he was my favorite uncle. My father also cried through the entire service. Mahlon was his older and only brother and they were very close. After Uncle Mahlon's death, my father seemed to be a broken man. He looked sad and very tired. He had nothing to say to any of us. I would often see him trying to blink back tears. My mother was very concerned about his mental state and thought he possibly might have a nervous breakdown. Some of the church members were dropping by and they would pray with him and my mother. My parents were going through a lot with Ann Marie being pregnant, Richard and me rebelling, and dealing now with two deaths in the family.

Ann Marie's baby was due to arrive in a few months. I remember vividly the day I suspected she might possibly be pregnant. Carol, Ann Marie, and I were having hot dogs for lunch one day, and she became very sick, throwing up. The next morning she was still throwing up, which continued about a week or so. Carol and I decided she should take a home pregnancy test, and the result was positive. Ann Marie had started hanging out with Terry, a neighbor down the street from us, a few months after we decided that we no longer would be attending the Mennonite church. She was also very upset with how they treated me on communion Sunday. Terry was a member of Goshen Mennonite church as well as most of his siblings and mother.

It was a total embarrassment for my mother and father when they were told the news. My mother was so upset that this had happened to Ann Marie. Terry had taken advantage of their daughter. Ann Marie was not ready to have a baby; she was only nineteen. One evening as I was coming in from shopping, I saw Terry in the family room with my parents and overheard his conversation with them. He was asking them for forgiveness and also wanted their permission to marry Ann Marie. My father started quoting scriptures from the Bible pertaining to sex before marriage and continued to preach to him about the awful sin he and Ann Marie committed. I heard bits and pieces of his lecture to them. He ended saying, "Romance, love, and sexual desire was designed by God within the bounds that he set up. They are beautiful and holy, but it is for husband and wife to enjoy this love that He created for us."

Terry was one of six children. His mother joined the Goshen Mennonite Church when Terry was about twelve years old. His father did not belong to the Mennonite church and never attended with his family. I remember his mother on many occasions asking the congregation to keep her children in their prayers. They were always disobeying her. I do recall hearing screaming voices coming from their house often. I would also hear a lot of cursing. I knew Terry had a very bad temper, and he was always getting into trouble at home and school. I really was concerned for my sister's future with him.

The night after Terry's talk with our parents, I asked Ann Marie, "Do you really want to marry Terry?"

Ann Marie replied back, "No, but Mom and Dad said that what I need to do is marry him," and she went on to say she did not love him and that he had forced her to have sex with him. Ann Marie then added, "Terry really doesn't want to get married, either." She continued to tell me how she got pregnant. He and his sister, and a boyfriend of his sister got drunk one night, and they forced Ann Marie to drink; then they checked into a motel. We both cried and

I told her to let me know if he ever hurts you. A week later Mom, Ann Marie, and I were planning the wedding.

They had a beautiful outdoor service at the Wheaton Regional Park with many church friends and family members. The reception followed with a sit-down dinner. About an hour into the reception, I overheard someone say that one of Terry's siblings had spiked the punch with vodka. I could not believe it. I went into the kitchen asking if that was true and was told, "Yes." I glanced around the room and noticed some of the Mennonites looked kind of tipsy. I heard lots of laughter, which was not like the Mennonites; they were always very quiet and reserved people.

I went over to my parents and told them not to drink the punch in the bowl. Dad said with a big smile, "I am really thirsty today; maybe because it is very warm outside. The punch is really good. I already had two cups, and I was thinking about going back for the third."

"No Dad, no more punch. I will get you some water," I told him sternly. I walked over to the punch bowl and brought it into the kitchen and poured the rest of it down the drain.

I was really concerned about my parents driving so I offered to drive them home. I never did tell them about the liquor in the punch. I was so upset with Terry's sister but was too afraid to say anything because I did not like any confrontations, especially with his older sister. Terry's sister who spiked the punch was a member at Goshen Mennonite Church. Her pastor is the one that banned me from attending their youth group socials.

My mind drifted back to when I was banned from the socials. I knew then what the youth were doing outside of church gatherings, but I never did tattle on them or gossip. The reason why I was so hurt over the pastor's decision was I knew I was living a clean, godly life and so many of the other youth were living a sin-filled life.

Many of the Goshen youth were very wild and rebellious when away from the church people. They were involved in drag racing, smoking cigarettes, cursing, and seeking pleasure since most of them came from non-Mennonite homes.

Chapter 17

DISTANT LOCKS WAY

By the time I was eighteen, a girl becoming a woman, I had pretty much divorced myself from my family, with the exception of Richard and Ann Marie. My parents were visiting other churches outside the Washington, D.C./Baltimore area. I was told by one of my Mennonite friend's parents that since the communion Sunday when I was denied communion, they did not feel comfortable at our mission church. They knew that my older siblings and I were never going back to Gaithersburg Mennonite Mission Church again. They were hoping that if they found another Mennonite church, not in the same conference, we would eventually come back to the fold.

They were very disappointed when we assured them that we never wanted to be a part of the Mennonite faith again. My mother and I kept our distance from each other since she could not bear to see her once obedient, vibrant daughter turning into a very argumentative and rebellious daughter. Dad started making negative comments about my appearance. He would remind me always by saying, "Sharon, you are totally ruining your natural beauty. Why are you making your eyebrows so thin? That lipstick is going to fade the natural beauty of your lips." He went on to say, "I can't believe you cut your hair so short. You don't look like the Sharon I once knew." Dad had become very judgmental toward us since we no longer were practicing the Mennonite faith.

Christmas was approaching within a few weeks so Richard and I decided to buy a Christmas tree. We brought it home and set it up in our family room. We spent hours decorating the tree. Later that evening as I sat admiring the colorful tree, Dad appeared in the doorway with a very disgusted look and spoke with a very angry voice, "I don't believe I am seeing this in my house!" As he approached the tree, he picked it up and carried it to the sliding door and threw the tree outside with lights and all on it.

My heart had already checked out with my dad. One day he told me that I was going to hell and that I was a very bad influence on my younger siblings. I could not believe I was seeing his horrible actions and he blurted out, "You guys need to leave within one month!"

Richard had bought a television for his bedroom a couple months prior to Christmas, which greatly displeased my parents. As I was still in disbelief about what had just happened, my father was walking out the door with Richard's TV in his arms. My dad also threw the TV outside. I ran to my bedroom and cried until I heard a knock at my door. It was Richard; he had just arrived home from his date with Carol. He asked, "Where is the Christmas tree?" Still crying I said, "Dad threw it outside!"

Richard was furious saying, "I can't believe he did that!"

I added, "Richard, he also threw your TV outside."

Richard left my room but in a few minutes he was back, informing me, "The TV is not outside."

We never did find the TV. We were very disappointed in our dad's actions and knew we had to leave sooner than later. We found out later that Dad had buried the TV in the back yard.

Richard, Carol, and I signed a year lease on an apartment in Gaithersburg.

Carol and Darren's father passed away due to a heart attack a few months before. Carol decided she wanted to move in with us, since she and Richard had been dating for three years.

My mother was very sad to see us leave. Actually, I noticed Mom had aged maybe ten years since that horrible communion Sunday. She and I lost something very special that we once had together. I never understood why my parents did not come to my rescue on that horrible Sunday morning. Our love and trust was broken. I no longer spent time with her just talking. We said goodbye to our parents and our younger siblings. My youngest sister began to cry as I said goodbye to her. She was only two years old. Lisa was a surprise baby. Lisa thought I was her mother since I always spent a lot of time playing with her and spoiling her. When I was out on dates with Dale and didn't come home until 11:00, sometimes later, Lisa was waiting at the door for me.

I was sixteen when my mother announced she was expecting another baby. She was forty-two years old. I remember the day she told us the news. I was very upset with her. I said very disgustedly, "Mom, you are too old to have another baby. You already have six children." I could tell she was very disturbed by my comment.

The Mennonites do not believe in birth control, so I am surprised she didn't have more children because I would hear them making love almost every night when I was younger. Their bedroom was adjacent to my bedroom, and I could hear the headboard banging against the wall and I would hear moaning and my dad telling her how much he loved her. The air vent was next to my bed. One night I heard them climaxing together. I heard their loving words to each other. My dad was saying, "I love you, I love you, Eva Lynn, I love, you!!" Then I heard Mom's words telling Dad, "Oh honey, you are so good!"

They had such a special love. It turned me on so much. I would reach for my pillow and begin humping it. I was telling my pillow also how much I loved it. Apparently, my mother and father enjoyed making love to each other. They also enjoyed hanging out together after dinner, sitting on the sofa holding hands and discussing their busy day. When Dad did not work late into the night, he would lend Mom a helping hand in the garden.

I remember one day when I was, perhaps, only fourteen years old, and I was in their bedroom sneaking around looking for my Christmas presents and I came across a book titled *Love Making for Christians.* I browsed through it very quickly, and it was showing different positions to make love. The different positions were very fascinating to me. My thoughts went back to the night I was babysitting several years ago when I thumbed through my neighbor's book entitled, *How to Have the Best Sex with your Spouse.* I wanted to see if oral sex was in the Christian book, but I could not find anything in it regarding that disgusting stuff. I noticed a position that I could do with my pillow. I ran to my room and locked the door and began humping my pillow; I added a second pillow.

I would have multiple orgasms. I knew I was addicted to this awesome feeling.

Chapter 18

BROADWAY PATH

Out of sight from my parents, I started living a very different lifestyle. I was drinking and occasionally smoked marijuana to numb the pain stemming from being tossed out from my church and family. After moving into the apartment, my life changed tremendously. I was making dinner, doing my own laundry, and paying bills. I now had many responsibilities that I never thought about before. I was holding down a full-time job, going to college at night, and working my part-time job on Saturdays. I was now totally on my own at eighteen years old.

Our first weekend at the apartment, Richard, Carol, and I decided to have a party. We had about forty people packed in our apartment. We had a full keg of beer and everyone was dancing to the Beach Boys music. We had black lights on and were loudly making small talk while the beer was starting to take effect. We danced the night away with the Beach Boys. Dale was the best dancer there. I asked him, "Who taught you how to dance?"

He said, "I learned from going to the Mount Airy Friday night dances."

After the last person left, Richard and Carol had already checked out for the night, Dale took my hand and led me to my bedroom. He opened the door and we jumped in the bed with all our clothes on. We cuddled in each other arms until I started feeling dizzy. The bed was spinning so fast. I was getting nauseated. I thought oh no, I could not hold back. I was throwing up all over Dale and me. Dale slept through all of it.

The next morning he woke up before me, and I heard him say, "Lift your arms up, Sharon; you got sick all over yourself and me last night." He took all my clothes off as I was trying to wake up.

He carried me to the bathtub. The water was already running with the bubbles rising to the top of the tub. He graciously placed me in the tub and began pulling my hair back off my face. His touch sent shivers down my spine. He then ran his hands down my breasts and my stomach trying to get all the dinner from last night off of me. I began laughing. He leaned over me, and whispered, "Sharon, may I get in with you?" I thought he was only kidding and then he asked again.

"Hmm, I don't think the tub is big enough for both of us," I whispered. I really didn't want Richard and Carol to hear us. I have never even thought about taking a bath with anyone else. This was so crazy the request he had just made to me.

I said, "No I don't think that is a good idea."

I closed my eyes, hoping he would just leave but I then felt his foot on my leg. I opened my eyes, and he was coming in with a big grin on his face. He was staring down at me with a look of desire. He asked me to turn sideways so he could lie next to me. I obediently turned my body sideways, causing the water to lap over the edge of the tub. My heart began pounding. I could feel his body next to me.

"Oh, the water is so warm," he commented, "and so is your body," as he kissed my shoulder and neck, everything else was hidden under the bubbles. I thought to myself, is he going to make love to me in the tub? He started rubbing my neck with his hands.

I asked him, "Have you ever done this before?"

He said, "No, I just like experimenting new things with you. I love you so much, and I just want to be close to you and hold you and make you feel wanted by me."

Dale seemed very experienced in the love-making department, and I desperately wanted to learn more. I felt down deep in my soul that God no longer was in control of me. Satan and Dale were in control! Anything he wanted, he got. I never said no. I thought I might lose him, and I then would be all alone. I did love him. I loved that he cared about me. He is mine and I am his.

With that thought, I turned to him and began kissing his mouth tenderly, thanking him for taking care of me. I was beginning to feel comfortable with him next to me, but then he quietly suggested I get on top of him. I began humping him, and he moaned as we climaxed together.

I cried out, "Oh baby, baby I love you so, so much."

He put his arms around me and said, "Wow that felt so, so good." He then got on top of me, holding my hips and thrust me into another awesome climax.

I was waterlogged when we finally returned to the bedroom.

Dale asked, "What do you want to do now?"

I replied, "Let's take a nap." We stayed in bed the entire day, talking, snoozing, and making love.

Monday morning came and I had recovered from our first party. I was starting a new job today; working fulltime at Cramer Video as an office manager. I was the only employee besides my boss.

My boss traveled a lot, so most days I was alone greeting customers and doing office duties.

My boss was traveling one day when Dale called and asked if I would like him to bring me lunch.

I answered very quickly, "Oh, that would be wonderful."

After we ate our lunch at my desk, he asked me if I would follow him to the bathroom. Without hesitation, I followed him. He closed the door and locked it. He guided me to him. He unclasped my bra, and it dropped to the floor. His hands held my breasts, and he started nibbling on my nipples. I moaned with great pleasure. He started kissing me with wet lips. He kissed my breasts all over. I could feel the heat from his body which was so warming to my chest. He sat down on the toilet and I straddled him as he continued kissing me.

All of a sudden I was brought back to reality when I heard the main outside door open. We jumped to our feet. I tried to remain calm as I quietly said, "Stay in here" as I flushed the toilet, turned the exhaust fan on and stepped out of the bathroom and closed the door.

It was a customer that stopped by to see my boss. He left a tape with me and asked, "May I use your bathroom?" I know I turned many shades of red as I replied, "Oh no, you don't want to go in there. Please, let me show you another bathroom."

After the customer left, Dale came out laughing uncontrollably, saying, "Good job; well done, Sharon."

The first two years of our relationship were very sexually driven. We could not get enough of each other. I lost my virginity at age eighteen. I was ashamed and disappointed in myself. I will never forget the night we went parking. It was the night I lost my virginity. We started making out in the front seat. Dale was a fabulous kisser. He knew how to use his tongue quite well. On the other hand, I felt like a clumsy kisser, my teeth were too big for my mouth and were always getting in the way. We had been to a Friday night dance and were drinking wine all night. We had the car radio on and were listening to, "Let's Get in On" in the background.

We were enjoying just kissing and holding each other. His hands were roaming all over my body: in my hair then to my toes. I was so turned on. His tongue and my tongue are twisting and turning together. Dale whispered to me, "Hey Sharon let's get it on." Before I knew it we were in the back seat making out. It was no dry humping with a pillow this time; it was the real thing. After it was over, I felt ashamed of what had just happened. Satan definitely had me by the hand.

One year after experimenting with sex I was told by my GYN that I was pregnant. I was devastated. I confided in Richard, and his response was "Sharon, you are too young and not ready for a baby; you need to consult with Planned Parenthood." I thought this meant giving my baby away when it was born. Dale also was not ready to start a family. He pushed the abortion option.

"What is an abortion?" I asked. I knew it didn't sound comforting to my ears.

He replied, "It is like having a D and C." I didn't know what a D and C was, either, so I thought I would make an appointment with Planned Parenthood.

For days I cried and I wanted so much to tell my mother I was pregnant but was so scared to bring it up since she warned me often "do not give away your virginity." I was terrified thinking about ending my baby's life. She would remind me by saying, "You don't want to end up like Ann Marie or your friend Donna. You need to save yourself for your husband. Sharon, you need to keep yourself pure for your husband, and God will always bless your marriage."

Thoughts of Donna entered my mind. About four years ago I had invited all my Washington/Baltimore District Mennonite girl-friends, including Carol, to a slumber party at my house. I was celebrating my acceptance into Lancaster Mennonite High School. I was fifteen years old. We were all having a fun-filled night with pillow fighting and playing pranks on one another when Mom appeared in the doorway announcing I had a visitor upstairs. I ran upstairs and saw Donna standing in the kitchen with tears in her eyes. We embraced each other what seemed like eternity as she was telling me how much her life had changed. She shared with me news about her baby, Michael who was nine months old at the time. She had Michael midway through her tenth year of high school. She confided in me that she had planned on giving him up for adoption, but after she held him for only a minute and as the nurse was taking him out of her arms, she cried and said she could not give her baby away. Donna dropped out of school and became a fulltime mom at age sixteen.

My mother always taught me to be chaste (Titus 2:4-5). "It is a calling to personal character, to moral purity, to sexual purity and it's one that is extremely important" she would always say. Mom would remind me often, "You need to honor God with your body. Your body belongs to God, so always be respectful by keeping your body pure. Be strong, not weak; never give your body away unless it is with your husband."

Mom was not at all well educated, but she was biblically educated. She shared and planted many valuable lessons from the Bible (the Book of the Law) to her offspring. I remember in devotions we often read Joshua, chapter 1. The two versus that she stressed to us were verses 8 and 9:

> Do not let this Book of the Law depart from your mouth; meditate on it day and night, so that you may be careful to do everything written in it. Then you will be prosperous and successful, Have I not commanded you? Be strong and courageous. Do not be afraid; do not be discouraged, for the Lord your God will be with you wherever you go.

The next day I made an appointment with a counselor at Plan Parenthood. The lady assigned to me was definitely a kind, caring person. I told her how I was brought up in a Christian home and that I could not talk about this to my parents. I did not tell her I was raised Mennonite because at this time in my life I was anti-Mennonite. I was still blaming the Mennonite Church for my division with my mother and father. I missed having a relationship with my parents so much, and I was beginning to get very discouraged about life since I knew down deep that Satan had me wrapped around his finger; God was totally not involved in my life anymore.

My counselor had mentioned in one of the meetings that she was going to ask me many questions and my answers would help her to know me better. She wanted the best for me. She did tell me there were alternatives, other than an abortion. Well, now I was well aware how failure to guard my thoughts and doings—a failure to keep them pure, can lead to this personal ruin and devastation. I could not murder this baby growing inside my womb. That is insanity to kill your baby. She informed me that having an abortion is not killing a human being. It is still a fetus at six weeks and is not yet fully developed and did not have a heartbeat. She handed me literature to read about the abortion and, after some thought, I made the horrible decision to have the abortion. The next day after the abortion, I cried all day.

Dale's mother called and asked me, "Is it true you are pregnant?"

"No, I am not pregnant," I answered.

Her reply was, "Well I heard from one of Dale's friends that you are! What are you going to do about it, Sharon?"

I told her again that I was not pregnant.

She finally said, "I hope you are not lying to me."

I said goodbye and hung up the phone. I slept for two days. I did not want to see or talk to anyone.

Chapter 19

BROKEN LAND PATH

ale's mother, Diane, was an only child, and I thought she was very spoiled. She was very pretty and had the most beautifully shaped legs. She would wear really high spiked heels and short skirts. She wanted to be in control of everything. She didn't think I was good enough for her son. Sometimes I would think to myself, take the spikes off and come down to my level. Try to get to know me. I really care about your son, and I am a good person. She started inviting me to Sunday dinners and I would accept her offers. One night she asked me if I knew Sherry Schwan, and I said, "Yes, I met her in second grade and did not see her again until the tenth grade. Why do you ask?" I said.

Diane said, "Sherry is Dale's cousin." I felt so embarrassed. I was wondering to myself if Sherry said something to her about me.

Diane asked me, "Do you like Sherry?"

I replied, "Well I never hung out with her in school since she always thought she was so much better than most of her classmates. She was a cheerleader and was very conceited." I told Diane what happened in second grade about Sherry telling me I was a copycat and that December 11 was not my birthday.

Diane said, "Sharon, that is not Sherry's birthday; her birthday is in January but her mother wanted her to start school a year early so she had her birth certificate changed." I could not believe what

I was hearing. Sherry back then, in second grade, knew it was not her birthday and thought I was lying also. I thought to myself, the truth shall be known eventually.

One Sunday night for dinner I was told we were having turkey hearts. I had never had turkey hearts so, of course, I wanted to try one. It was so tender and the flavor was delightful. I went back for seconds and thirds and then everyone started laughing at me.

I asked, "What is so funny?"

"Sharon, you are eating mountain oysters (pig testicles)," chuckled Jack (Diane's significant other). I thought I was going to get sick, and I excused myself from the table. They would serve me wild game like groundhog, turtle, squirrel, rabbit, and possum, but I could not believe they would feed me pig testicles. How cruel, I thought to myself. I did not think this was funny! It was a long time before I accepted another dinner invitation from his mother. I think she was very jealous of my relationship with her son. She referred to me as a long, stringy blonde haired gal from Laytonsville. Actually, when she met my parents, she could not believe Dale, her son, was dating a girl from a Mennonite upbringing.

I was beginning to think often about the abortion. I was being haunted by it, so I tried to stay busy with working, going to college part-time, and seeing Dale whenever possible. Through staying active, I did find a measure of happiness, but it was like putting a band-aid over a wound. The band-aid felt more comfortable, but the wound never healed. I was beginning to think that I would always have to live with this wound as part of my punishment for not keeping myself pure for my husband which was embedded in my mind since my early teenage days. I shared with Dale one day how horrible I felt inside about aborting our baby. He was very sympathetic about my feelings. We would cry together. He was crazy about me, at least that is what I thought because he was so jealous of guys talking to me, and he didn't want me to have any guy friends.

One weekend, Dale and I decided to have a pool party at his house. His mother and Jack had made plans to go to Las Vegas for the weekend. We invited twenty-plus friends. I had not met Dale's most recent friends. I was in and out of the pool, socializing and making sure everyone was having a good time.

My friend, Patty, and a few more of my friends arrived much later that night and as I was returning to the pool, I noticed all the outside lights were off. Thank God for a full moon. I could see heads bobbing in the water.

"Dale, where are you?" I shouted. I heard a voice coming from the deep end, "I'm over here." I walked over to the sliding board and looked down into the water and noticed he had no swimsuit on. I saw a naked girl swimming underwater away from him. I glanced around the pool and many couples were making their own little whirlpool around themselves. I demanded Dale to get out of the pool, and with my cigarette in hand, I began searing his chest. I was furious that he had been skinny dipping for the last hour with all of his naked friends.

Dale grabbed me and I yelled, "Let go of me; you are disgusting and I hate you!"

He gazed at me and said calmly, "Sharon, please don't act like this."

I replied, "I am so, so hurt."

I was so mad, big scalding tears were flowing down my face. I ran to my car but saw that I would not be able to leave since I was blocked in. I had to go. I did not want to stay with him that night because I did not feel like ever making love to him again. He was not good for me. He was not deserving of me. I felt totally broken. I would have never been involved with being naked and making out with just anybody in the pool.

I slept on the sofa that night. The next morning Dale approached me, asking for forgiveness. I saw the burned marks on his chest and began crying. I was so sorry about losing my temper and pulled him close to me and we cried in each other arms. I was sorry and he was sorry. My hazel eyes and his brown eyes stared at each other for a few seconds until he invited me to his bedroom. Hand in hand we walked to his bedroom and locked the door. There were a few bodies crashed out on the floor.

We undressed each other and he carried me to the bed. His lips were moist as he kissed my neck. He caressed my breast with his hands and began sucking on my nipples. I was in awe; he was a fabulous lover. But, of course, I had never made love to anyone else. He was my first. I was completely at the mercy of his expert touch.

We were making love many times a day when we were together—on the kitchen table, under the kitchen table, on a golf course, or a football field, on the mountainside, or in a ditch. I was in love with sex; I was addicted. Thinking back to my early teen days, I am sure that hearing my mom and dad making love and saying sweet things to each other during their lovemaking had something to do with my addiction. I felt so loved when I was engaged in lovemaking. I wanted to have what my parents had with each other. I wanted to be loved like my dad loved my mom. I knew, though, that the Lord was not blessing my relationship like He was blessing my parents. God was missing from my life totally. There was no praying, no joy in my life, and no reading His word or worshipping Him.

Looking back to a few years before, I remembered my English teacher from Lancaster Mennonite High School had a discussion with me and a few friends about sex. She confided in us that she had only one addiction and it was sex. She had been a very rebellious teenager and drifted from her upbringing and became involved with non-Mennonite boys and indulged in sex many times a day. She went on to say that God did give us this wonderful gift; God did create love, but we need to keep ourselves pure for our husband. She pleaded with us not to make the same mistake she made.

Reflecting back about a year ago, the day after I lost my virginity, it was a hot Saturday afternoon when Dale and I decided to take a motorcycle ride to Hagerstown. As we were approaching the top of South Mountain, Dale steered the bike to the side of the road. We were enjoying the view of the valley and also each other's company. We started making out on the mountainside with cars flying by us. Holy cow, I thought to myself, we are making love on top of a mountain, but I didn't care. I was enjoying every minute of it. I wanted him here, now, in the ditch! I had the same addiction as my LMHS teacher had, sex and more sex. There was no more humping my pillows. I never revisited my pillows again unless to sleep or cry in them.

I also was not visiting with my parents and siblings. My parents were absent from my life due to my worldly lifestyle. They would often let me know they were praying for me. They would also let me know how I was living a very sinful life and possibly might miss Heaven as long as I continued to worship Satan. My parents also reminded me often how I had broken their hearts.

I was neglecting Ann Marie, who now had two children and was living with her abusive husband. One night she called me begging me to come get her. Ann Marie's husband just beat her up. I got dressed and picked up her and her two small children and took them to a domestic violence shelter in Silver Spring. Ann Marie stayed in the shelter for a few weeks.

Ann Marie was told by our parents that she could come live with them but under their rules only. This meant she could not bring her TV. She would have to wear dresses below her knees, and she would have to go to church with them on Sundays. Our parents at this time had moved further out in the country, and Ann Marie thought she would be very bored not being able to walk into town. Ann Marie never learned how to drive. She had a fear of driving, and I think it had a lot to do with her accident when we were younger,—the day she drove the car through the neighbor's fence and almost destroyed the above-ground pool.

After some thought, I advised Ann Marie to apply for welfare and she was accepted. The state provided her an apartment surrounded by low-income families and people on welfare like herself, a single parent scraping by in poverty and despair.

Chapter 20

SUMMER WAVES PLACE

After living with Richard and Carol for a year, I decided not to renew my lease with them.

My friend Patty (from middle school days), the gym friend who accidentally shot an arrow at me, was looking for a roommate. We had reconnected a couple of years out of high school. We were at a ballpark in the summer of 1975, playing softball for the City of Gaithersburg. We exchanged phone numbers and became softball buddies.

We signed a one-year lease on another apartment in Gaithersburg. We were excited and we had so much fun decorating our apartment. Patty had brought her antique dining room furniture. I purchased new living room furniture, and a burnt orange shag carpet. We were very happy with our new home. We would entertain friends on the weekends. I was still dating Dale, though he was spending more time with his guy friends. He told me one night that his mother thought we were spending too much time together and thought he should back off seeing me every night.

Early one morning, I received a telephone call from my cousin, Melissa. She informed me that Dale had spent the night at her neighbor's home with a girl that apparently worked for the same company as Dale. She went on to tell me that they had been seeing each other for about a month now. I did not totally believing my cousin. How could Dale do this to me? I thought he loved me; at least that is what he was telling me.

The next evening I went over to my cousin's apartment complex and saw Dale's car in the parking lot. I cried myself to sleep that night. It was the first time in my life that my heart felt so much pain. I confronted him with having an affair with my cousin's neighbor, and he begged me not to be upset, telling me that he still loved me. I told him that I needed some time to think about it. A week later Dale came to the ballpark where I was playing softball and saw me sitting with a really handsome guy; he became very jealous. Dale called me over to his car and begged me to let him spend the night with me.

I said, "No, it's over. I will never be able to trust you again."

On occasions, Patty's police friends would hang out at our place after their shifts ended. One Friday evening after a ballgame, I came home and walked into a poker game. I noticed some of the police had some clothing missing. Patty announced my arrival to her friends, "Hey guys this is my roommate Sharon." They said "Hi, come join us."

I asked, "What are you guys playing?"

Someone yelled, "Strip poker."

I ran to my room and put on earrings, bracelets, socks and a belt, knowing that I was not the best poker player. We played for hours. I lost everything I had added but no clothes came off. A couple of the police guys were dressed down to their boxers. Patty's friend, Elaine was dressed down to her bra and jeans. Patty's police friends were very entertaining. They would have us laughing hysterically about their stories arresting people.

Patty was very attracted to her police friends, but the one and only she really loved and hopefully would marry one day was Wallace. Wallace was six feet three inches tall with dark hair and very handsome. He was always smiling and always wore sneakers, even with his police uniform. After dating Wallace for almost a year, he proposed, but Patty knowing that he had an affair with another woman, told him she would have to think about it. While she was thinking about marrying him, Wallace was informed by the woman he was having an affair with that she was pregnant. When Wallace told Patty the news, her heart was broken.

Patty, over the next year, dated a couple of other policemen, but she could not get over her true love, Wallace. I could never understand how Wallace could hurt my friend. Patty had many great qualities. She was very pretty. She was sweet and so caring. She had the most stunning, beautiful, sky-blue eyes. Patty had so many friends. She had never changed from the girl I met in gym class seven years ago. Thinking back seven years ago in middle school, Patty came into my life at a very crucial time since I was very discouraged about life; I was tired of being so different and feeling lonely. I wanted my life to end. Patty reached out to me with compassion and kindness, a day I will never forget. She gave me hope that there are people who do care. She accepted me as a new friend with open arms.

Patty really does care about her friends. She would give you the shirt off her back. Who would have known that a wayward arrow would lead me to a new best friend, forever. We did everything together. She would include me in all her outings with her friends, and I included her in my circle of friends. Patty had many older siblings. She was one of ten children. One of her older siblings was having a Halloween party. I decided to go with Patty and a few other friends. What a blast; it was the best party ever. Cathy, Patty's sister-in-law was very welcoming. She introduced me to so many people. We danced and danced most of the night. There were boob flashing contests.

Patty said, "Sharon, I know who is going to win!"

I replied in a surprised voice, "Who do you think?"

"Cathy, of course," smiled Patty. "She always wins. Cathy is a 40DDD."

I often thought of my crazy life. I was doing anything I so desired to do. I was experimenting with marijuana, drinking, smoking cigarettes, and now I am contemplating flashing my boobs. How crazy!

Chapter 21

LOW TIDE PATH

The year living with Patty went by quickly. There were many fun times! We decided not to renew our lease since Richard and Carol had split up and Richard was looking for a room-mate. After I moved in with Richard, I decided to buy a new car as the apartment rent was much lower. I traded my car in for a new MG midget convertible. I had been so embarrassed to drive my old car since it had been spray painted in big black letters "PUSSY GALORE."

Patty had awakened me one morning after discovering it as she was leaving for work. I ran to my car and could not believe what I was seeing. Who would do a thing like that? I did not have any ene-mies at least that I know of. The only person I ever shared myself with was Dale. I called Dale and asked him if he sprayed painted my car, and he said, "Definitely not," and I truly believed he was telling me the God's honest truth.

I asked him, "How do you remove black spray paint from a car?" He knew everything about cleaning a car. I also knew he had respect for cars (since he worshiped his car), and could never be abusive to a car. He would clean his car every day. He replied, "Sharon, I am on my way." I really did miss seeing Dale. It had been about three months without him in my life, although I knew he was not good for me since he could not be faithful to me. A few weeks later I found out who spray painted my car and was totally confused, since she was a very good friend—or at least I thought she was.

Dale and I missed each other tremendously so we decided to start dating again. I had a very forgiving heart, and I forgave him for his unfaithfulness. I remember as a child it was instilled in me that we should always be forgiving, as our God is very forgiving. Dale promised me he would be committed to me from that day forward. Growing up I remembered my parents always modeled commitment to each other. I also thought if you are boyfriend and girlfriend you need to be committed to each other and not be involved with anyone else. I was beginning to feel confused about relationships. Can you love more than one person?

In the two and a half years that we had been dating, I never was involved with another guy, except for the guy he saw me with at the ballpark, but that guy was just a friend of my brother's.

Anyway, it was a new day and a very sad day for me. Dale informed me that his mother's significant other bought a restaurant/bar business in Frederick, and he was offered the managerial position. I was not happy about this offer to Dale. I knew that this would require him to work nights and weekends. I also thought about the environment being surrounded with drunks. Dale always did worry me when he drank since he became very flirtatious and lost all self control, like most people do. I pleaded with him not to take the job, but he informed me that he had already accepted.

Looking back on my life with Dale (two and half years) the memories that I had with him were mostly spending our free weekends drinking. We would drink our weekends away by visiting multiple bars. On Sundays I would stay in bed fighting nausea and raging headaches from Friday and Saturday hangovers. One Friday night, we decided to visit with our friend, who was a bartender at a Bar/Grill in Mount Airy. After a few drinks, I mentioned to Dale that George (the kid that bullied me in middle school) was sitting at the table next to us. Dale jumped up and wanted to knock him out; Dale was my protector these days and no one was going to hurt me.

I was starting a new job as an accounting clerk for Digital Satellite in a few days. I was told that I would be sharing an office with my supervisor. He was about fifteen years older than me. Jeremy was a great boss, so easy and understanding. He did not smoke but allowed me to smoke in the office. One afternoon after lunch, I lit up a cigarette and the running tape for the adding machine caught fire from the burning cigarette in the ashtray. Oh what a scare! I had a big blaze going in the office, and he just laughed. Jeremy was very shy but a kind man. He tried too hard to be funny, but we did laugh a lot.

A couple months later, it was my twentieth birthday, and Jeremy invited me to lunch. After lunch he asked me if he could drive by his house to pick up the mail, and I said, "Yes, of course, you're the boss!"

When we arrived at his house, he said, "Sharon, come on in, I want to show you the house," so I followed him in. When we approached the master bedroom, he pulled me close to him and whispered quietly, "Sharon, I want to make love to you," as he grabbed me around the waist, pushing me toward the bed.

I blurted out, "No, this is not right! You are married!"

Jeremy threw me on the bed, putting his finger over my mouth and said "Shhhhhh!"

He murmured, "Your body turns me on. Your body is so sexy. I want to hold you close and make love to you, please, please, Sharon," he pleaded with me. He put his arms around me and began kissing me on the lips and said, "I can't persuade you to make love to me?" as he was unzipping his pants with one hand.

"No!" I again blurted out.

I jumped up from the bed and ran out of the house and started walking down the street. He pulled up beside me and asked me to get in the car. I did not want to but it was about ten miles back to the office. I climbed in and he turned to me and said, "I am so sorry for everything; please do not tell a single soul." Jeremy continued saying, "Sharon, I will promote you to a higher position and give you a pay raise, if you say nothing at all about this, ever. Please, Sharon, do not tell anyone!"

After this, I was not comfortable being in the same office, and asked if I could be moved to another room; Jeremy agreed. Another four months went by and I saw a job posting for the engineering department, working directly for the VP of software engineering. The requirements were typing 60 wpm and taking dictation at 40 wpm. I knew I was not qualified for this position, but I thought of going back to night school for a crash course in speedwriting and that is what I did. I did not pass the typing test but somehow I was offered the job. Jeremy gave me a fabulous reference, how I was a fast learner and very easy to work with.

I became the social butterfly since my desk was now in the open hallway. I had everyone stopping by my desk to chat. My job was to support the entire engineering department. I was given many responsibilities and was so overwhelmed. My pay was increased by twenty percent. I was also in charge of scheduling after-work activities. I decided to play softball in the upcoming co-ed fall league. In my first game I was assigned starting pitcher. No one knew that I had ever played softball before, and I was striking out batters left and right. My peers were so impressed. I became very popular overnight. After the game we went to happy hour at a pizza place. We made a habit of partying after every game.

Dale became very jealous and broke up with me. He did not like me hanging out with men from work. During one of our breakups, I started dating a preacher's son. He was a technician, working in one of the labs. We would hang out after work, have dinner, or go hiking until twilight approached. Barry was an outdoorsy kind of person. I agreed to go camping in Gettysburg, Pennsylvania, one weekend with him and a group of his friends. It was so cold that weekend. We pitched our tents, started a fire and talked and laughed the night away with the help of booze and pot.

It was about twenty degrees outside, but with Barry snuggled up next to me, I had forgotten about how cold I was. His body was so warm with all of his heavy winter gear on. He touched my chin with his warm hands and kissed me goodnight and said, "Do you mind if I lie close to you tonight?"

I answered softly, "No" and I returned the kiss, and within minutes he was snoring.

Lying awake I started thinking about how Barry would never touch me in a bad way. We held hands and kissed mostly on the cheeks. This was our fourth sleepover, and he never asked me to have sex with him. He did tell me in one of our talks that he wanted to save his virginity for his wife. I truly understood where he was coming from because I once had the same desire, and it was embedded in me from my mother to save myself for my husband.

The next morning, we opened our tent to find five inches of snow on the ground. How beautiful the snow looked on the tree branches. For the first time in four years since I left the Mennonite Church, I started thinking about the non-Christian life I was living. Barry was the only friend from work that I confided in about how I was raised Mennonite.

We often had discussions about losing our salvation and we didn't know quite where we stood with God. He and I knew it was sinful how we were living. We did not have a personal relationship with Jesus. We often talked about rededicating our life to Jesus. Down deep I wanted to live a Christ-like life again. I wanted to do what was right. I was tired of the partying.

That night I talked to God for the first time in almost four years, asking Him how this happened to me; living in a sinful body and having a sinful mind? His reply was (not an audible voice), "You have forsaken me. I am not your friend; Satan is. You never talk to Me anymore." I had not opened my Bible in almost four years. My life was becoming so chaotic. I was neglecting Ann Marie. My parents had given up on asking me to come and visit with them. I really had no friends who were truly believers. I was easily influenced to smoke a joint or snort some cocaine if a friend asked me.

One night Barry invited me to hang out with him at his house. I accepted and he told me that he was attracted to a church friend back home, but wanted to know if I would consider getting married to him someday. He went on to say, "Sharon, I could spend the rest of my life with you. You are everything that I want. I want to share everything that is mine with you. All I want is to give you all my love." He continued, saying, "Sharon, you need to give me an answer tonight. Will you be my girlfriend and future wife someday, yes, or no?"

I was so torn between Dale and him. I could not commit myself that night. He was really upset, but I knew down deep that I was not ready to make a commitment to him. Also, there was another guy on the horizon who was interested in me. Barry and I tried to keep our distance from each other. I would often think to myself that he would be the perfect husband, a preacher's kid. How closer to God could I get?

I also thought about Darren, how I rejected him and now he was planning a wedding in January, the next month. I knew I was going to regret one day for not going back to Darren. My mother warned me I was going to be really sorry one day for breaking up with him. The first time I ran into Darren with his wife-to-be, I actually felt a tinge of jealousy. I knew that Darren was happy, and I was going to support his decision to marry his girlfriend Karen. She seemed very much in love with Darren. I was very happy for both of them.

Springtime had arrived and I was looking forward to our softball games. We would play into the twilight hours. After a fun-filled game of softball one evening, a few of us from work decided to go for pizza and beer to celebrate our win. After a few beers, I got up to leave and lost my balance and fell, knocking over a chair. An engineer friend offered to drive me home but I refused. He walked me to my car, and talked me into putting my convertible top up. I agreed.

As I was driving home, very carefully, I lost control of the car, and it flipped off the road down an embankment. Apparently, there had been roadwork earlier that day and the side of the road had a twelve-inch drop. The car rolled a couple of times. I managed to get out of the car.

A few minutes had gone by, and I saw strangers walking toward me, asking, "Are you okay?" I nodded my head yes. I put my hand on my head and felt a big bump. I heard sirens.

The strangers asked me, "Do you have anything in the car you want us to take out?"

I replied, "No."

After the police searched my car, a cop approached me and put handcuffs on me, saying, "You are under arrest." I was in disbelief. I had been drinking, but I didn't think it was a reason for an arrest. The police officer showed me four baggies of marijuana, mostly seeds.

My brother had been using my car, and apparently he had left the baggies in the glove compartment. I said, "Please, officer they are not mine." He laughed and walked me to his car. I cried the entire way to jail. I was scared out of my mind. As they were taking my fingerprints, preparing me for a cell, I pleaded with them to let me call a friend. I also mentioned a few police friends of Patty's. Wallace came to my rescue. He talked with the commissioner, and they agreed not to lock me up. Instead, I was allowed to make one phone call to get bail money. Dale came to my rescue with $1,000.00 and I was released.

I was charged with aggressive driving, driving under the influence of alcohol, and with possession of marijuana. I had to go to driving school and AA classes. I also had to hire an attorney to represent me in criminal court. It is such a small world; the attorney representing me knew my parents. My attorney's wife was a social worker who handled cases for my foster sisters and brothers.

At my court hearing, my attorney told the judge that the marijuana found in my car did not belong to me. Of course everyone in the courtroom started laughing. My attorney went on to tell the judge that I was employed by Digital Satellite and Shady Grove Lumber and worked very hard, that I was not a pothead, and that this was my first offense. He went on to say that he knew my parents and they were wonderful Mennonite people.

The judge looked at me and asked me, "Are you a Mennonite?"

I replied, "No, but I used to be."

He then said, "Sharon, I am sure your parents are hurting so much about all of this," and I nodded my head in agreement. The judge dropped all the charges, and I thanked him as I sat down.

My mother called me a week later after my trial and informed me that she and Dad were praying for my soul and pleaded with me that it is never, never too late to come home to Jesus. "Sharon," she cried, "please, surrender your life to Him and, live your life for the Lord again." My parents were heartbroken when they heard of my arrest. My mother always wanted the best for her children, and she was blaming herself for my wayward behavior and sinful lifestyle. I reminded her that this was my life. I was the only one that was going to have to answer to God for my doings in life, and I was responsible for all the wrong choices I had made, not her and Dad.

"Mom, I am truly sorry for breaking your heart, but I want to assure you that you and Dad were the best parents, and I will be just fine. Do not worry about me," I said as I hung up the phone and cried. I felt so shameful for putting my parents through all of my hell.

Due to my arrest, my employer took my secret clearance from me, so I could no longer work on top secret documents. The arrest made it to the president of the company, and he informed me that I should look for another job. I had been miserable for the last three months at Digital Satellite. One of my bosses, Joe, VP of communications, was very difficult to please. He would call me into his office every morning and dictate several letters to me. I disliked shorthand. Actually, I used the speedwriting technique. By the time I was ready to type the letters, I had difficulty understanding what I wrote. He would get very nasty and slam books around on his desk when I asked him a question about something he dictated to me. He asked the president of the company to hire another secretary for him. I ended up reporting to her.

One of my engineering friends told me that Amerisat was hiring in Germantown so I scheduled an interview the next day. I met with the personnel director, Harry. He was a nice-looking man with blond hair and blue eyes. We talked about an hour. I was given a typing test and was told I could start in two weeks. A few days after I gave my two weeks' notice, I was approaching my desk when I heard the new secretary talking on the phone with Joe. He had called to say his wife had committed suicide, and he would be taking some time off. I have to say I did feel sorry for him, although he was a very difficult man and probably drove her to kill herself.

Chapter 22

SCENTLESS WAY

My new job as an administrative assistant to Mike Stern, Director of Program Management for Amerisat was easy, and my workload was so light compared to my last job. Mike was a very pleasant man, with a great sense of humor. I had only one guy to report to and only him to support. I met new friends and would hang out with them after work if I had nothing planned with Dale. Dale joined us if he wasn't working at the bar. We would often go to happy hour and have a few drinks; then maybe go to dinner or to a movie. I enjoyed my new friends at Amerisat, especially Harry, the personnel director. I would hang out with him and his friends on occasion.

After being employed with Amerisat a few months, I was promoted to a program analyst and moved into my own office. Another girl also applied for this position. I knew a few of the women in my department were very jealous of the men stopping by my office and hanging out. One day I noticed no one was stopping by. For a few days there was a bad odor coming from my office. I thought to myself, is this smell coming from me? The smell was coming from below my waist. I put my head down to smell myself and thought, where is this smell coming from? I brought in a lemon-scented spray and would spray several times during the day.

One morning I walked into my office and could not bear the fishy odor. I went to my boss and told him that my office smelled like dead fish and asked him to move me to another room. He walked with me to my office and we took everything out of the desk drawers. In the bottom drawer to the very back, was an opened can of tuna fish! Our mouths fell open in disgust. Who would do such an awful thing like this to me, I was thinking to myself. Harry felt so bad for me, knowing that I had been embarrassed about the smell coming from my office, so he agreed that I could put a sign on my door saying "The horrific smell was coming from my drawers (my desk drawers), ha, ha! An opened can of tuna fish was planted in my bottom drawer." Everyone that walked by chuckled but knew I was very upset. My boss said, "Sharon, I know you don't find this funny today, but later in life you will think about it and laugh about it with your children."

Harry invited me to happy hour that same day with some of his friends. I had a couple glasses of wine. We talked and laughed about life. Harry loved people and life. He was always smiling and had a sunny disposition. He was my sunshine. I was very attracted to him. He was seven years older than me, but again I just wanted him for a friend. I could trust him. He was divorced and had one daughter. I think she was about five years old. After happy hour was over, he invited me to have dinner with him. I had other plans with Dale so I declined.

The next morning when I arrived at work I was given tragic news. Harry had been killed in a head-on car accident. He was on his way home from dinner, and a drunken driver crossed over into his lane and hit him, killing him instantly. Harry's life ended too soon. He was a devout Catholic, and I know he was ready to meet his maker. I was devastated. How senseless to have a wonderful friend taken from you because of a drunken driver. He was the only really nice guy that I loved talking to except for my boss, Mike. Mike was a wonderful Jewish man. His wife loved him very much and would call him at least five times a day. I really had a lot of respect for him. He and his best friend, Joe Carluccio, would on occasion come to happy hour together but have only one drink and go home to their wives. Mike and Joe were comical about being old married men, but they adored their wives and children.

Richard and Carol were now planning a wedding. Richard informed me he will be moving out in a couple of months. I decided to lease an apartment closer to my new job. In order to pay all my monthly bills I would work overtime if needed; I was living alone and my rent had doubled.

Usually it was the proposal department that kept the midnight oil burning. I would sometimes work all night; then go home, take a shower, and return to the office for another full work day. I would do this often. Dale was working nights at the bar so he was pretty much there until two or three in the morning so there was no time for us during the week. One night, after a few hours of overtime work, a guy friend shouted, "Hey let's smoke a joint, let's party!" So there we were congregating, about six of us, two guys and four girls, smoking a joint in the parking lot. One of the girls yelled, "Let's strip down to our underclothes, and run around the building for the fun of it!" That is what we did, while laughing the entire time.

I was having fun with my new group of friends at Amerisat. I saw Dale only on Friday or Saturday nights if he did not have to work at Pete and Benny's bar. Pete and Benny's was a rock-and-roll, hole-in-the-wall kind of place with a mechanical bull in the center of the dance floor. It was a kind of place where anything goes. There were many different types of people that were regulars, such as motorcycle gangs, hippies, rednecks, even a few businessmen, and I can't leave out the animals. Yes, believe it, I have seen donkeys, dogs, cats, and even a few rats come and go.

My relationship with Dale was on a roller coaster ride most of the time. I would often catch him in lies. He would say he was with a friend, but that friend would call me and ask me if I knew how to get in touch with Dale. I was getting phone calls from friends saying they saw him making out with a barmaid at Pete and Benny's. I was told by one of the barmaids that there was a bed on the second floor. One night I decided to surprise him at Pete and Benny's. When I arrived there, I was turned away by one of the bouncers. He said I was not allowed in. I thought maybe he knew that Dale did not want to get caught. I left crying. I really did love Dale. Why did he have such a hold on me? I was so confused and broken.

Dale was beginning to drink heavily and sometimes he would get very violent. One night he totally went off on me and began pushing me and yelling at me because he said I was flirting with someone at the bar. I disagreed with him, and he then became very angry banging my head against the wall. I remember collapsing to the floor and the next thing I saw when opening my eyes was Dale, crying apologizing for hurting me.

Reflecting back on Mount Airy Friday night dances, he would frequently get very jealous of guys looking at me or talking to me, and he would actually get in fights with them. I remember nights he would go home with a swollen lip and/or a black eye. I would often think to myself that Dale should not be drinking since he loses all his faculties. My mother would often say that alcohol and drugs can keep a person from thinking clearly and it also keeps them from growing up. I can remember as a child visiting with my friends from the community who had alcoholic fathers. They were very abusive with their language and not very sociable. A few of my friends were afraid of their fathers. "When a person does not have to look at life through realistic eyes, how can he possibly be mature about his personal efforts?" Mom shared with me after a visit with one of my friends from the community. I saw firsthand the destructive consequences that drinking does to a person at a very young age.

Dale would disappear for a few days. I would not hear from him and, thinking he had someone else. I would get very depressed, and I began staying to myself a lot.

It was time for my annual well woman's checkup. I remember six months ago I was told by my GYN that I had gonorrhea. I had gone to the doctor because I had an unusual secretion of mucus coming from my vagina. The test came back positive that I had contracted a venereal disease. I asked the doctor what causes this, and he said having too many sex partners. I told the doctor that I have sex with my one and only boyfriend, Dale. The doctor replied, "Dale apparently passed it on to you." I confronted Dale asking him if he was having sex with other girls, and he couldn't believe I was accusing him of this. He went on to say that I could have picked it up from a dirty toilet. I believed him.

My exam again came back positive for the disease. The doctor put me on a very strong antibiotic and told me Dale needed to start taking the antibiotic also. We were passing it back and forth. I was so confused how we could be passing it back and forth for almost a year now. I had not been involved with anyone else, and Dale was telling me that he also was not having sex with anyone else.

It was Dale's twenty-second birthday. He had just moved in with me since his mother was involved in a new relationship, and he felt uncomfortable living at home. I wanted to surprise him with his favorite meal, stuffed pork chops. I informed him before leaving for work that I had something special planned for his birthday and asked him if he could be home by 7:00 p.m. He replied, "Of course, that should not be a problem, but if it is, I will call you." I rushed home from work to prepare the dinner. On my way home I had stopped and bought a bottle of wine and wrapping paper for his gifts. I was so looking forward to a very quiet and romantic evening. I had everything done and was waiting for him or a call, but I heard nothing. It was going on 8:00 p.m. so I thought I would make some phone calls.

I called Pete and Benny's and they told me he had left hours ago. I called some of his friends, and no one had seen Dale. The last call I made was to his friend, Brian, and was told he was there. Dale came to the phone and I asked him why he didn't call me to let me know he was not planning on spending his birthday with me and he replied back, "Sharon, I am on my way home now." I waited until 9:30 and still no Dale.

I drove to Brian's and knocked on the door. A complete stranger that I have not seen before answered the door, "Hi, can I help you?"

I asked him, "Is Dale here?"

He said, "Yes, and who are you?"

"I am Sharon, his girlfriend.

"Oh really, then I don't think you want to go in there," he whispered.

I pushed by him and walked into the main room and looking to my left through the doorway of a bedroom, I saw Dale with a girl. I was devastated and ran out of the house. The stranger ran up to me and asked me if I was okay to drive because he saw how angry I was. Dale then ran out of the house and asked me what I was doing there. I told him not to bother coming home, that he and I were through.

I cried myself to sleep that night but about 2:00 a.m., I was awakened by Dale. I had locked the bedroom door just in case he did come home. The next thing I saw was the bedroom door coming down and Dale walked through the doorway with a disgusted look on his face (I always had a table light on when I was sleeping alone). I was not emotionally stable enough to even talk about what he had just put me through. I was still devastated. He jumped into bed, lying next to me, and turned to me to say how sorry he was that he got drunk with his friends and lost track of time. As he was murmuring his apologies, I smelled liquor breath on him and his hands smelled so disgusting; I guess you would say his hands smelled like love juices.

I sat up in bed and yelled, "Go brush your teeth and wash your nasty smelling hands! How dare you come to my bed smelling like that!" Although I was thinking to myself that Dale never promised me a rose garden. I slept on the sofa the remaining hours that I had left, since it was Saturday morning, and I needed to be at my part-time job in a few hours. As I was waiting on a customer, a young man came up to me at the register and handed me a dozen roses. I smiled and said, "Who are the roses for?" I was thinking maybe Dale had sent the roses to me since he knew how upset I was with him.

He replied, "I brought them for you." I did not know this man, but I had seen him in the store before. I was checking him out as I was thanking him, and I suddenly remembered he was in his car several times when I was leaving the parking lot after work. I remember one day he followed me back to my apartment. He was stalking me. He was probably in his early thirties. After this encounter with him, I became more cautious about my surroundings. I would check out the parking lots at work and home. I was very observant about everything going on around me.

One Friday afternoon, I decided to go home for lunch. As I was approaching my complex, I noticed a young lady running from the building. About ten minutes later, I saw smoke billowing out from my neighbor's window. I called the fire department, and the police arrived within a couple of minutes. I was asked by the police if I saw anything unusual and, I of course, told them I saw a woman running from the building. I described her face to them. I had to pick her out of a lineup a few weeks later. Come to find out, she was a sister to one of my co-workers at Shady Grove Lumber. She had been charged with arson. Her husband had been having an affair with my neighbor, and she was furious and wanted revenge.

I was being threatened by several of my coworkers at the lumber store, saying that if I continued as a witness on this case I would be very sorry one day. I never did go to my supervisor regarding this threat. A month before the trial date, my supervisor approached me and said, "Sharon, you are fired!"

I asked him, "Why?"

He replied, "You have been taking money from the cash drawers, and we know it is you."

I denied his accusations but he did not believe me. I sternly said, "Please believe me. I did not take money from the cash register!" I could not believe what I was hearing from my supervisor. Apparently, it was Amy, a friend of the girl that I was testifying against, taking money out when she was covering for me on my lunch breaks. I was told by my supervisor the money stolen had totaled about $500.00. I was very upset of being accused of something I didn't do. I started trembling and wanted so badly to confront Amy about this, but I was walked out the door with my supervisor and was told to leave the premises.

That night I prayed for strength to help me get through this difficult time. There is so much evil surrounding me. Why are people so cruel? I have never in the last few years, since leaving the church, seen so much jealousy, hatred, and evil in my life. I know I had lived a very sheltered life as a Mennonite, but I could not believe that people could be so hurtful. My prayer ended in, "Please God, help me forgive those people who have done me wrong, including my own family and church family, who have cast me out. I am not a bad person, God. You know what is in my heart. I really do want to live a clean life, but it is so hard since most of my friends are non-believers and are very worldly. Please, Lord, keep me safe since I have a few people extremely angry at me."

I was feeling very lonely. After I had caught Dale with a girl on his birthday, I decided to accept his apology and I did forgive him, but I knew that I needed to move on from him. He just could not leave the drinking alone. All of his friends drank and used drugs, so I am sure that is one of the reasons he could not be faithful to me. I knew in my heart and soul that drinking was very destructive to any relationship because when drinking you are not in control of your thoughts and doings.

I was missing my family. I had not visited with my parents since the day I moved out. Four Christmases had gone by without seeing them or any of my relatives, except Richard, Ann Marie, and Melissa. I know I have been a very big disappointment to them. I was beginning to hate life. I didn't like the person I had become. The life I was living now was not a healthy life. Smoking, drinking, and not going to church was taking a toll on my body and spirit.

A few weeks out from my twenty-third birthday, I received a phone call from Ginny a co-worker, who worked in the proposal department. She was inviting me to a social her department was having at her supervisor's apartment. I accepted her invitation. They had so much food and many bottles of wine and champagne. They were celebrating a big contract win! After the last person was saying goodbye, I turned to Bob, Ginny's supervisor, a nice looking African American man to also say goodbye. He asked me to stay since I only lived the next building over. He poured me a glass of wine and sat next to me. We started talking about our families. He had been raised Southern Baptist and said he noticed there was something different about me.

I asked him, "What is so different about me?"

He said, "You are very humble and down to earth. You are not like most of the girls at work."

I confided in him about how I was raised Mennonite and the struggles I was having about losing my family due to lifestyle choices which my family could not accept. I went on to say that I had messed up my life. My character had been ruined due to all the sins I have committed. I poured out my heart with tears streaming down my face.

He said, "Never give up hope that someday you will make a difference in the world." He told me that I was blessed with knowing the Lord and that I am a child of the Heavenly father and that God will never leave my side. "You know, Sharon," he gently added, "believe it or not, God has been your strength, getting you through all life's ups and downs."

Bob continued to tell me that there was something very special about me. I was capable of doing anything I set my mind to do because I had the right attitude, I was kind, and I was a very driven, hard worker. He added, "Sharon, you are a very attractive girl. I am not saying you should move to Hollywood, but you have many gifts, so go get 'em, Sharon." He continued, "Stop being so critical of yourself, and I want to challenge you right now to put your complete trust in God."

He paused for a few seconds and added with so much enthusiasm, "God is a loving God, and He wants you to be happy. You do matter; you have gifts that He gave you while you were still in your mother's womb. You need to find your purpose in life and His plan for you. For some reason the pain of the past can be easier to believe than the promises of God's future plans for us. I am encouraging you to find the courage to believe wholeheartedly in God again. People, including family, have been tearing you down mentally. Let it all go. God wants you to have a new beginning with Him. Are you ready? God is ready now to give you all His great and precious promises."

I thanked Bob for his wonderful encouragement and gave him a big brotherly hug and said, "Goodnight."

Walking home that night, I asked God to forgive me for living such a sinful life. I felt like I had just been cleansed of my sins. I was always taught that God is a very forgiving God, and I felt so close to Him at that moment. I felt His presence and His love for me again. I was beginning to understand why I felt lost because I did not feel loved by Him; I was very angry with God because He allowed people to mistreat me.

There was a full moon, and it was a very clear, crisp and dry night. The stars seemed like they were winking at me. As I was walking home, I saw a huge animal tied to the lamp post of Dale's friends' apartment building. As I got closer I saw that it was a mule, and he smelled like liquor. The mule was drunk. I approached my building and saw Dale's car. I went inside and Dale was asleep on the sofa. I was surprised that he was there since I had not seen him for a few days. I tried to awaken him to tell him about the mule tied up but could not arouse him. The next morning, leaving for work, I saw Dale with a friend trying to get the mule in a friend's car. They had the back seat out of the car. Apparently, someone at the bar dared Dale and his friend to get the mule drunk and take him for a wild ride!

I thought about what Bob had said to me last night. I wanted to make some changes in my crazy life. I called my mother and asked how everyone was doing and said, "Mom, I miss you and Dad!" Mom was so surprised and happy to hear from me and she invited me to come for Sunday lunch. I accepted.

Chapter 23

SILKEN LEAF WAY

Sunday morning I got up early and attended church service for the first time in five years. I attended a Baptist church down the street from my apartment. The people were so friendly and were very welcoming. The message was "Become who God designed you to be." The minister asked us to turn to Ephesians 2:10 and read together the verse, "For you are God's own handiwork, recreated in Christ that you may do the good works that God predestined for you."

After we sang a few hymns, the minister began his message by saying, "You are God's special handiwork, equipped and anointed to be the person God has called you to be! The Bible says in Psalm 139 that God knew who you were before you were ever formed in your mother's womb. You have special gifts, abilities and talents, and God has a unique plan for your life.

The enemy (Satan) may try to make you think you have to conform to the opinions of others, but if you are secure in who God made you, then you can resist those outside demands and pressures that try to mold you into something you're not. As you continue to grow in your relationship with the Lord through prayer, worship, and fellowship with other believers, you will gain confidence in the Lord which will free you from the opinions of man and allow you to be the person God called you to be!"

I thought to myself this message was meant for me. Bob and I were talking about this a few evenings ago. "God," I prayed silently, "please show me how to use my gifts to fulfill your plan and be a blessing to those people around me. I really want to have you again in my life."

After the benediction and as I was leaving, a young woman came over to me and extended her hand and invited me to a single woman's social the following week. I asked for her phone number and said I would call her.

I got in my car and started driving to my parents for Sunday lunch. For the first time in many years, I searched for WRBS, the Christian station that I listened to religiously when I was a child. I began crying, and thinking that I really did not have any friends who are truly believers. I began feeling so ashamed of myself for not even opening my Bible in years. It all just clicked. My life was in shambles because I was not living for the Lord; no praying, no daily devotions, no Christian friends, or going to church. As a child, I was very happy and cheerful because I had the supernatural spirit (Jesus) within me, and I wanted to be the best person I could be, like Jesus. I remember as a child I would hear Mom say often, "Without Jesus in your heart you will be a miserable person."

I arrived at my parents' home where colorful silken leaves blanketed their driveway. Getting out of the car, I thought how wonderful it would be to spend some time with the family again. As I walked inside, I saw my youngest sibling, Lisa, walking toward me. She was now almost seven years old. She had very long braids down to her waist. She was wearing a long dress to her ankles. My other sister, Kerri, had her hair up in a bun with a large white covering that had white ribbons hanging from it. My mother was dressed in a very dark dress almost to the ankles. I saw she was wearing black stockings and black shoes. I know I looked very surprised because my father came over, but when I went to hug him, he backed away and just shook my hand.

I said, "Dad, I need a hug from you." He replied, "Sharon, we have changed our membership to a more conservative conference, and their belief is not to have contact with anyone but our people and then we only exchange greetings with a Holy Kiss."

"But Dad, I cried, I need a hug." I continued talking, "I have missed you and Mom so, so much."

Mom walked over to me and shook my hand, saying, "Sharon, it is so nice to see you again. You have lost so much weight." She continued, saying, "Are you eating?" I thought to myself, I am sure it is the cigarettes, instead of biting into something sweet, I would light up a cigarette.

I stood in the kitchen with my long lost family, almost in tears. I could not understand why they had become so different, so plain. My siblings Steve, Dennis, Kerri, and Lisa acted like strangers. My sisters looked so different in their dress attire. More and more Mennonites today are wearing jewelry, makeup, and dressing worldly. Between the strict and more liberal extremes there are many shades of practice. My family looked like Amish people.

They looked very sad for me, I was thinking. We sat down for lunch, and Dad asked the blessing, thanking the Heavenly Father for the wonderful day he had given us and thanking Him for keeping me safe. He asked the Lord to reach into my heart and help me to see the need for Jesus in my life. Dad ended his prayer saying, "Mom and I so long for Sharon to follow You again. In Jesus' name, Amen."

After lunch, I helped with the dishes and asked Mom if I could turn on the radio to WRBS, the Christian station. She replied, "Sharon, we do not believe in radios anymore, but if you want to sing or listen to gospel singing, we do have a record player."

The visit did not go as well as I was hoping. My father seemed to be very ashamed of the way I was dressed. He said, "When you come to visit in the future, and we hope you do, please wear a dress below the knees. Do not wear pants or we cannot welcome you in our home. Keep the makeup off your face, and please do not wear jewelry."

I left there thinking I didn't belong to this family any more. The love they used to have for me had dissipated. They surely did not show me unconditional love. They were being very judgmental and hurtful with their words and actions. I felt like getting drunk or smoking a joint. I wanted to numb this pain I was feeling; I felt like an orphan. Driving home after my short visit with my family, I felt so unloved and unwanted. I started thinking about Dale. He was the only person in my life that gave me fulfillment. I always looked forward to our nights together making love. Everybody needs to feel loved by someone, and if you do not have God in your life, you will find love elsewhere. Dale was my inspiration to go on.

Back at the office the next day, I felt very sad and lonely. I felt drained of all my energy. I kept thinking about my visit with my parents. I really didn't know them anymore. They were so different from the parents I knew as a child. My dad did not show me his enthusiasm about life, and he was not the warmhearted dad I remembered. My mother did not have much to say to me, and my siblings just sat and stared at me, looking at me from head to toe.

My hurting heart was crying out for my parents' love again. I wanted to be accepted again. I wanted to have a relationship with my family again. They were not mirroring God's love, which creates a longing in even the coldest of hearts. Actually I felt like the prodigal son returning home, and I was hoping to be embraced with so much love and attention. I wanted to see smiling faces, but I saw only sadness and that exacerbated my pain and guilt.

A few months ago my company went through another organizational change and moved my wonderful boss to another location. One of my new department heads (Jim) came over to me and said, "Where is the letter I gave you about two hours ago?"

I responded, "I'm almost done. I will bring it to you in a few minutes."

As I was leaving his office after putting the letter in his inbox, he made a comment, "Hey, Sharon, you know if you could type with your butt, you could really produce some work!"

I turned around and said, "Hey, Jim, you are forgiven for that nasty comment."

Later he came out of his office and pinched me on my buttocks as I hurried down the hallway. I was hoping that someone would see his awful gesture and report him to Human Resources. I never understood why the men gave me a hard time about my butt. I was never told or never did anyone even make comments before about my butt until just recently. The men would often give me a pat on my butt. I knew this was inappropriate and knew it was sexual harassment. I also knew if I reported them to personnel they might lose their jobs, but I was too nice and didn't want to get them in serious trouble. Actually, I felt like they were my family. I would just put up with their silly actions.

One morning I was picking up my copies from the Xerox room, and one of my coworkers came up from behind me and grabbed me and said, "Sharon, you are built like a brick house," and he began singing the song to me.

In bed that night, thoughts were racing through my mind about the men at work. If they knew I was raised Mennonite, would they be treating me this way? I thought about my mother's comment about me losing a lot of weight. I was always on a diet because I did notice other women in my office had a much smaller bottom. My diets consisted of starving myself, then I would get comments like, "Sharon, you look dehydrated/sickly."

I started putting up a wall around myself. I felt separated from my family and, most devastating, I did not feel close to God anymore. I started shutting people out, both friends and family. I didn't trust people anymore; they were so hurtful. Even family members were throwing stones at me saying how bad I was that I am a sinner and am going to hell if I keep living this sinful life. I started keeping to myself. I would go to work, go home, and stay home. Being sociable did not appeal to me anymore. I was hurting and worn out from years of many painful memories of wounds caused by relationships and the church.

My cousin, Melissa (she never joined the Mennonite church), made a comment to one of our mutual friends that I had no friends. The reason she thought I had no friends was because I never brought any of my friends around her because she was so spiteful. Once I had a Tupperware party, and the entire evening she kept putting me down. She would say or do horrible things about anyone that I cared about. I remember a couple of years ago, Ann Marie called me really upset saying, "Sharon, I walked over to Melissa's apartment with the children and she ignored me. She would not talk to me."

I tried to console her by saying, "Don't let it upset you, God will take care of her in due time." I continued on to say that God opposes the proud but gives grace to the humble. God loves you and you are much better than proud Melissa."

Ann Marie at that time in her life really had only one good and caring Mennonite friend, and it was Jeannette Goodman. Due to Ann Marie's limitations, Jeanette was there for her to take her places and always had a helping hand with the children. Our mother also helped as much as possible.

I was at a very difficult place in my life. I was torn which life I wanted to lead. Is it going to be with God or the world? I knew the Mennonites didn't accept me. They did not even want me when I was a believer, a godly Mennonite girl. None of my church family or my extended Mennonite relatives ever tried to contact me since that horrible Communion Sunday. I had no contact since that Sunday with any of my Mennonite friends. I was associating only with the world, and it seemed that they were my only family now.

Reflecting back to the last days of my Mennonite life, what I needed from the church and family was encouragement and unconditional love. They were so critical of everything I did, very judgmental. I could never fully understand why I was not served communion, which has left the biggest wound. No one, not one minister has ever apologized about that Sunday. If the church really cared and loved me the way Jesus loves me, how could they treat me like that? Wow, our Jesus does love. He did not waste His time mocking others, nor their religious trappings. He loved, really loved. It didn't matter if you were a Pharisee or a prostitute; disciple or a beggar; Jew, Samaritan, or Gentile. His love held itself out for any embrace. Due to the church not accepting me as a believer, it tore my very close- knit family apart and the church family.

Back in ninth grade when I had a vision to become a missionary and travel around the world helping the unsaved find Christ, I remember praying every night for my classmates that they didn't end up destroying their lives by using alcohol and drugs, and I knew I never wanted any part of that kind of life, and look at me! I am living that life right now! How did this happen to me? I am now lost also, just like my classmates were. The Mennonites chased me away. My vision to be a missionary was no longer in my heart. I felt hopeless and discouraged about life.

The next several months, I remained to myself. Dale was noticing a change in me because he would ask me often if everything was okay. One day he asked me, "Why are you so quiet? Is something bothering you?" I replied, "I feel so lonely. I feel like nobody cares about me anymore." He responded back, "I care about you, Sharon, and I always will. You are very special to me!"

While spending Easter morning with Dale on the Potomac River, he proposed to me while we were fishing. He said, "Sharon, will you marry me and spend the rest of your life with me?"

I, of course, replied, "Yes, I would love to be your wife." In the back of my mind I knew that since I gave up my virginity to Dale, in God's eyes and my parents' eyes, I would need to marry him. We celebrated our engagement with a bottle of champagne. That night lying on the sofa with Dale next to me was so awesome. I felt so loved by him once again. He was a wonderful lover. I was ready for this big step in the marriage adventure since I am very adventurous and was ready to have children (my dream was to have at least six children). I was twenty-four years old.

We snuggled up next to each other. I ran my hand through his silk-like hair. I loved his hair. His hands played with my hair, and we rubbed each other's heads. Dale kissed me passionately and held me so tight. We curled up on the sofa and discussed our wedding plans until we couldn't keep our eyes open. He scooped me up and carried me to the bedroom. I was exhausted. I don't ever remember being this tired. He softly whispered, "Goodnight, my beautiful wife, it's time for sleep; no more loving tonight. I am the luckiest man on this earth."

Chapter 24

ETERNAL RINGS PATH

I conceived the weekend Dale proposed to me, I am sure. Our relationship seemed like it had never been so good. He and I would spend every possible moment together, talking about the wedding and the arrival of our baby in seven months. We called each other several times a day and expressed our love for each other. He stayed away from the booze since I was not drinking. During this time, he would constantly tell me how sorry he was for all the wrong things he had done to me. I would always tell him, "I forgive you."

We could not get enough of each other. This continued about two months; then Dale stopped calling me every day, and sometimes he would not come home from work. He would stay out all night. The next day he always had a good excuse, like "Oh, Randy and I had too much to drink so we just stayed at Pete and Benny's." One night he didn't come home so at 6:00 in the morning. I drove to Pete and Benny's to find Dale and Randy passed out in the car with the engine still running. I knew if he didn't leave Pete and Benny's, our marriage would not survive this crazy life.

I had thought about calling off the wedding because Dale seemed like he was getting cold feet. But, in the back of my mind I was thinking about raising a baby alone, and that just seemed impossible to me. He was drinking more and not coming home every night. My mind drifted back to our meetings with the pastor who was going to marry us. In one of our counseling sessions, the pastor stressed to us that marriage is a commitment for a lifetime and asked if we were ready to be committed to each other forever.

Dale spoke up and said, "Do I have to stay with Sharon if she decides to go back living as a Mennonite, wearing her covering? What if she puts on 100 pounds; can't I leave her since she changed from the person I married?"

I sat there in disbelief what he just asked the pastor. My feelings where deeply hurt. The night before the wedding Dale brought prenuptial papers for me to sign. I could not understand why he even thought for a minute that I would be unfair and try to take what is not mine.

It was a very hot summer day on my wedding day, August 29. I was going to be walking down the aisle in about two hours, with Richard giving me away. I had asked my father to walk me down the aisle, and he refused. Mom and Dad did not even want to come to the wedding because they were totally against everything I was doing in my life. I had to coax them to come. There was a knock at the door. One of the bridesmaids hurried to the door. It was the limo driver. I was finally ready. I had my makeup on, and my hair was up on my head with pieces of hair enveloping my face. I was anxious to get the wedding behind me.

At the church, Boyds Presbyterian Church, as I was walking down the aisle with Richard by my side, I noticed my parents and siblings sitting on the side benches at the front of the church. Also, I noticed Darren, with his wife and toddler. My thoughts suddenly went back to the days with Darren. In my mind I often wondered what my life would have been like with Darren. I was really tired of all the drinking and the bar scenes. I knew Dale was being unfaithful to me. I saw Dale's grandfather sitting in the front pew, along with Dale's mother. I know they were not happy about their only grandson and son getting married to me.

Earlier I overheard Dale's grandfather saying to Dale, "Do you believe Sharon?"

Dale answered, "About being pregnant?"

"Yes, I don't think she is. She just wants you to marry her because she is afraid of losing you, and she sure does not look pregnant," I heard him say.

Walking closer to my parents I could see they had tears in their eyes. My mother had tissues in her hands. My siblings were staring at me. Mom had mentioned to me several weeks before the wedding that she didn't understand why I was spending so much money on the wedding. Mom did offer me $400.00 toward the costs of the wedding. I said, "Mom, that will not even buy my gown," and she replied, "We only gave Ann Marie $400.00 for her wedding." The Mennonite weddings were very simple, no flowers, no ring bearers or flower girls.

The day I picked up the $400.00, my mother said, "Sharon, one of your cousins told your aunt how much you were spending on this wedding. Your dad and I think it is not being good stewards of your money." She went on to say, "Why do you need an engagement ring/wedding band when you have the promise in your heart that you belong to each other?"

After the wedding, we proceeded to the reception hall. The band was singing "Mothers, don't let your daughters grow up to be cowboys." I glanced around the room and I saw there were a couple of tables of Mennonites, mostly my immediate family and a handful of cousins and an aunt. They looked very displeased. There were probably about 120 people at the reception which was a buffet dinner. Dale wanted an open bar, and he insisted the reception be the way he wanted it. I agreed to it since he was paying for most of it. I knew though, my family, would be very uncomfortable with the drinking and the rock-and-roll music.

After dinner was served, my family, along with my aunt and cousins, left. I walked outside with them and thanked them for coming. As my father was getting in the car, he said, "Sharon, you are going to have a very hard and sad life ahead of you. You are going against everything you have been taught."

I quietly said, "Dad, just pray for me and Dale. I need your prayers."

As my cousin Deidre was saying goodbye, she sadly said, "I can't believe what you just put your parents through."

I responded back with tears in my eyes, "I hope someday they will forgive me for all my rebellious ways."

The reception was nearing the end, but a lot of Dale's friends wanted to continue our celebration so we all met at Pete and Benny's Bar. There were so many drunks all around me. I was not drinking since now I was almost five months along in my pregnancy.

One of Dale's friends walked over and said to me, "Hey mama, let's see those big knockers!"

It happened so quickly, he jerked my dress down below my breasts. The people standing around me were totally in disbelief that Dale's friend would do something like that. I was so surprised that I stood up and said, "Dale, you are not going to say anything to this guy?" Dale just laughed it off since he had a buzz going.

Our honeymoon night did not go as well as I thought it would. Dale was very drunk and passed out shortly after we checked into our suite. I laid in bed thinking about how I had hurt my parents with having the open bar and the rock-and-roll band. They looked very sad and, were very disappointed, I am sure.

My mother still wanted to protect me from all the evil in the world. I remember there were times in my young Christian life when she protected me from the destructive, uninvited guest (Satan). She nursed the wounds left by the violent storms of life; my many worldly thoughts of wanting to change my beliefs (being Mennonite) when I was in tenth grade. My mother was not only a fabulous gardener outside (to the earth) but also gifted in gardening the soil of the human heart. She had planted in my heart seeds of love, joy, peace, patience, kindness, goodness, faithfulness, gentleness, and self-control. My mother weeded, watered, plowed and prayed every day that I would continue to live and set an example to my siblings and the world.

My mother knew God's word so well and would refer to the book of II Peter 1:5-11 and Jeremiah 10:10 "Cultivate faith, goodness, knowledge, self control, perseverance, godliness, brotherly kindness and love in your children. For as they are growing in these qualities, they won't be ineffective or unproductive and they will never stumble." My mother always wanted the best for her children. I can remember when I was fifteen years old and was very discouraged about life and being a Mennonite due to not having school friends, but I kept my faith and continued growing in the church because my parents gave me the right kind of attention; watering, weeding, and fertilizing my soul and showing love to me. My mother and I had a dynamic love for each other.

My parents willed me to live for God, and I did live for God, as a result of their love and attention. I wanted to be a missionary and spread God's Word to the whole world! I wanted everyone to know Jesus as their personal Savior. But, my wanting to spread the word about Jesus all changed after that horrible communion Sunday.

After tossing and turning for hours, it seemed, I finally knew that I needed to ask the Lord for forgiveness. "Dear Lord, I am coming before you on my honeymoon night, which should have been very special to Dale and me, but I am so unhappy and feel so alone. I feel very troubled about my life. I want so much to have a relationship with You and my parents again. I know my parents love me and are very concerned for my soul and, today, they saw with their own eyes that I am leading a very sinful life and possibly might miss Heaven. Please forgive me for not honoring my mother and father. Please, Lord, I need You in my life again. Please give me the courage to make some changes in my life. Also, Lord, please keep Dale and me safe as we travel to Nova Scotia tomorrow. In Jesus' name, Amen."

Chapter 25

SNOWDRIFT DOWNS

Patrick was born on January 13, 1982, a very cold and snowy morning. It was a long and hard labor, about thirty-six hours. The last six hours were very painful. I wanted to die. I begged for a C-section. While in labor, Dale received a message from one of the nurses that our friends, Dean and Terri, would like to join us in this big celebration; our first child was almost here. Dean and Terri visited with us in the labor room for several hours. Terri tried to help me with the contractions since she had been through this twice. I really wanted to be left alone, but she insisted she was there to help make it easier for me. I was screaming with pain, and Dale, Dean and Terri were just carrying on with their conversations, ignoring my cries.

I finally had to tell Dale to ask Dean and Terri to leave. I thanked them for caring and coming to visit, and Terri replied back, "That's what friends are for." The pain was becoming unbearable and I was still screaming for a C-section.

I delivered Patrick 8:30 the next morning. Oh what a beautiful little baby! He had a full head of dark black hair on a perfect rounded head with beautiful sky blue eyes. As the nurse cleaned him up and wheeled me into my room, I overheard people talking about a fatal airline crash. An Air Florida jet had gone down into the Potomac River. I learned about an hour later that some of my co-workers from Fairchild (Amerisat's sister company) were on that flight. I was devastated when I learned that Joe Carluccio, a good friend, along with six other of Joe's coworkers did not survive the crash.

I took eight weeks of maternity leave from work. I was looking forward to my time off to be with my newborn. Six weeks went by so quickly. Dale was gone quite often since he was still working at Pete and Benny's. One night I received a phone call from Dean, asking me if I knew where Dale was and I said, "Yes, he is working tonight."

Dean replied, "Dale and Terri are together at a bar in Gaithersburg." He gave me the name of the place and I jotted it down.

I said, "Dean, what are you trying to say?"

He then said, "Sharon, Terri and Dale have been messing around for quite some time."

I hung up the phone and cried. A few minutes later I called a neighbor to watch Patrick for about an hour. She agreed.

I pulled into the parking lot at the bar, walked in and saw Terri and Dale sitting together at a table. I thought Terri was my friend; apparently she was Dale's friend with benefits, as Dean told me on the phone. I turned around and walked out. I never did mention this to Dale. I was so afraid of losing him to Terri. Dale was a butt man and Terri was blessed with a big bubble butt. Thinking back before Patrick was born we often did a lot together as couples and Dale and Terri seemed overly friendly with each other.

I called Richard the next day and asked him if he would consider hiring Dale to help him in his booming business. I knew our marriage was not going to survive if he continued working nights, and sometimes I would not see him for a day or two. Richard came to my rescue and offered Dale a job with him doing renovations in a large apartment complex in Washington, D.C. Dale agreed to learn the profession.

The first day back at work, I was missing Patrick so, so much. I had a very hard time leaving him with a babysitter. I wanted to quit work and take care of my baby. I always had a deep love and admiration for babies and children; I guess maybe because I was around children all my life. I enjoyed taking care of my siblings. The first week back at the office was almost intolerable. The men in my department were slamming me with typing. One of my bosses stopped by my desk and said, "Tell me, Sharon, who taught you how to file?" He went on to say, "When you were on maternity leave, I could not find anything I was looking for. You need to take a class on filing!"

I replied, "I am so sorry; I will try to do better in that department!"

I was elated when Friday arrived. I had two days with my baby. I would hold Patrick all day long. Dale was also very attentive to Patrick, especially when he would start to cry. Dale would run to him to make sure everything was okay. Dale's mother Diane would stop by every day to make sure we were doing okay.

My weekends were spent with Patrick and caring for his needs. I enjoyed every minute with my newborn. I would carry my baby around the house with me as I did my house chores. I didn't want to leave Patrick on the weekends but Dale insisted we ask his mom to watch Patrick so we could meet up with his friends. I gave in to Dale's plea to meet up with his friends at a bar one evening. They apparently had popped some LSD earlier that night, and with the drinking, they were driving me to tears. I was missing my baby; I wanted to go home to be with Patrick. I was not having fun watching them trip on LSD. I begged Dale to take me home early, before the band even started playing.

Chapter 26

WOODLAND WALK PATH

he next year flew by. I was pregnant again. Dale and Richard's business was doing very well so Dale was able to save quite a lot of cash. One day Dale approached me and laid out $10,000.00 on the bed and said, "Sharon, we are going to start looking for a house tomorrow."

I gave him a big smile and said, "Oh Dale that is fabulous ... thank you so, so much for providing a home for our family!" My mind drifted back several years ago when Melissa, my cousin said to me in a conversation that Dale was a loser and would never be able to support a family or be able to provide a home because all he really cared about was partying. After he left the bar business, he was spending more time with me and Patrick. The drinking subsided during the week, but on weekends if we were to meet up with friends, the drinking was present.

We decided to buy the house that Dale's mother was born in. It was in the country and had an acre of land. The lot was very shaded with big, mature trees. Dale wanted to raise some chickens and maybe have a goat or calf. We completely gutted the first level of our house with Richard's help. We moved in six months later, a couple weeks after Nicole was born. I again enjoyed the next two months being home with my babies. Dale's mother would stop by every evening after work. Dale would stop by the local bar after work almost every day. I was beginning to realize that he had a drinking problem again. I would sometimes not see him until the next morning since I tried to go to bed when the children did.

Once again love had hurt me deeply. I was going to bed alone most nights. One night I lay awake thinking of my precious Patrick who, with his silliness, keeps me smiling through the day—and to see my sweet, precious little girl, Nicole, is to love her, giving her many kisses throughout the day. I have lost many precious things in my life, but I know that I will always have my children. My love for them is so intense, and I feel their love for me.

The next four years sped by with working full-time, then going home helping Patrick with his homework, preparing dinner, cleaning house, and grocery shopping. I was also painting the interior of the house in my free time. I would stay up all night until I finished a room.

Dale informed me one day that his business with my brother was not doing well. They were struggling to pay themselves. Summer was approaching, and I knew daycare was going to double because the children would be in daycare full-time. I called my mother and asked her if she would be interested in keeping Patrick and Nicole during the summer when she was available. "Of course," she said, "I would be so happy to help you. Sharon, you know we care so much for our grandchildren and hopefully they will learn some Bible truths when they are visiting with us. We love them as much as our own children, and we hardly ever see them. It would actually be good for Dad and me to have them around to help us with the chores."

Patrick and Nicole helped my mother in the garden and around the house. They looked forward in going to Grandma's house since she was always baking sweets and making fudge and peppermint patty candies for them. I picked up the children from my parents' house early one afternoon, and Nicole was standing at the door waving to me with a confused look on her face. I noticed the long dress on her and I thought to myself she was playing dress up with her aunts. I walked into the house and my mother approached me with a few more dresses. "Sharon, we were advised by the church that when Nicole is visiting with us, she needs to be properly dressed." I was speechless. I didn't know how to respond to that statement my mother just threw out there with the dresses. It was so hurtful that my mom could not accept my children for who they were. My children are not Mennonites.

I continued taking the children when I needed her to watch them. I decided not to say anything about their beliefs on how Nicole should be dressed. Summer was almost over, and I wanted to keep peace with my mother. I really looked forward to seeing her when I dropped the children off and picked them up. Mom was still my mother, and I respected her rules. One important message in the Bible that was instilled in me as a young Mennonite girl, "Children, obey your parents in the Lord, for this is right. Honor thy Father and Mother (which is the first commandment with a promise), so that it may be well with you, and that you may live long on the earth" (Ephesians 6:1-3).

Since my parents changed their membership to the more conservative Mennonite conference, it was hard to understand all their new rules, but I knew that I still needed to obey their wishes. Many of my relatives were dressing more worldly, although my parents and younger siblings were dressing more conservatively; almost Amish like.

Chapter 27

SATELLITE COURSE

The first morning the Patrick and Nicole were to be dropped off at daycare after spending most of the summer at my parents, I overslept. To make matters worse, I had awakened feeling that I had not slept at all. I had nightmares all night about getting fired from my job and then we would lose our home, since I did make a decent salary.

Dale had already left for work. I got dressed and the kids dressed and flew out the door. I dropped the kids off at daycare and drove like a crazy person trying to make it to work on time. My boss had told me he was tired of me being five and ten minutes late, and the next time he was going to fire me. He was documenting everything I did wrong: every misspelled word, if I didn't answer the telephone properly, and if I was a couple minutes late returning from lunch.

I was late arriving to work. Later the same day, I was called down to the personnel office. The director of personnel informed me that my boss was very unhappy with me and my performance. I was told I had one month to improve or I would be fired. I thought to myself, "Why does my boss dislike me so much?" I knew he was having an affair with one of the secretaries so I was thinking maybe he was trying to get rid of me so he could hire her. Actually, I thought about mentioning to the personnel director the comments my boss would make about my back side but I really did not want him to lose his job.

A month later I was called up to the office of the Vice-President of Software Engineering, Mr. Pindel who was my boss's boss. He asked me to close the door and have a seat. He began, "Sharon, I can't believe you have survived in the administrative field as long as you have. I have counted over ten typos in memos you have typed in the last six months. Don't you know about proofreading?" He continued on saying that I was going to be demoted, reporting to a manager instead of a director. Three weeks later at the office it was close to quitting time; my phone rang. It was Sue, the secretary to the Vice President of Sales and Marketing, Mr. Walter Howard. She told me that Walter wanted to see me in his office. I immediately got up and went up to the third floor, thinking all the way, why does he want to see me? Is he going to offer me a position in his department? I was almost running down the hall to his office. The door was open so I went in and he told me to sit down. He got up from his chair behind the desk and walked over to me with a very serious expression.

"Sharon, you were raised Mennonite?"

I looked away from him and said very quietly, "How did you find out?"

"Your dad is building me a huge patio, and he is doing a fabulous job but I can't believe you were raised Mennonite!"

Walt went on to say, "One day I came home early and your dad was packing up. We started talking about Amerisat and my position here. I told him that I was thinking about retiring soon but after the costs of this big patio, I am going to have to work for a few more years.

Your father interrupted me and said, 'Walt I have a daughter who works at Amerisat.'

I had replied, "No, Adam, there are no Mennonites who work there."

Your dad said, "Her name is Sharon Spring."

I said, "No, Adam, the Sharon Spring that works at Amerisat cannot be your daughter."

I confessed that I was raised Mennonite and Adam was my father.

Walter's reply was, "Sharon, I am so, so shocked! How did you get away from the Mennonites?"

I said, "Walter it is such a long story; maybe you should let my dad tell you."

I left his office feeling really embarrassed about my upbringing.

In just a few days after Walter found out about me, my men co-workers were treating me differently. There was no more patting on the buttocks or making remarks about my butt. I was not invited to happy hours after work. They stopped harassing me about my filing/typing skills and typos.

It was going on four weeks after I had been called into my boss's boss's office regarding being demoted, and nothing happened with that threat. One of my managers stopped by my desk and asked me about my family. I thought to myself does he know also about my past? He whispered to me and said, "Sharon is it true you were raised Mennonite?" I felt so embarrassed.

He continued whispering, "Sharon, can I ask you some questions? I really want to know what it was like to be so identifiably different. What was it like to be a young adolescent and dress so plain?" He went on to say, "Sharon, may I write your story?"

I replied, "No, I am going to write about my life experiences when I figure life out and I am going to tell it all, the good with the bad. Hopefully my story, my life experiences, will help many people not to make the same mistakes as I have made. I know you probably think Mennonites are still living in the dark ages, but I was taught values and how to treat people with respect, and to be kind and loving to all people. I have wonderful memories as a child. You'll never know how devastating this world is because you have never experienced the godly world. So, maybe I am very fortunate that I had a very different life because I do know right from wrong."

There had been a lot of gossip going through the office about my direct boss and a secretary. This affair continued for several months, until one day he asked her to come into his office and she would not listen, so he came out of his office and threw her up against the wall in front of my desk and threatened to have her fired. She went directly to the president of the company telling him what had just happened. He was fired the next day.

There was a saying, "as the satellite turns." This meant there were so many affairs going on behind the scenes. Many relationships were starting and ending almost every week. I can remember walking in on two people making out in an office. A few of the men even left their wives for their secretaries. It was crazy. There were so many after-hour affairs. Actually, I have to be honest, one of my managers and I became very close friends during a time that I was confiding in him about my troubled marriage. We would hang out after some of our happy hours, and gradually we started having lunch together which dead-ended since I was having so much guilt. Guilt for me is the ultimate punishment.

About a month after my boss was fired, I was promoted to an administrative position, reporting to the vice president of engineering. I was so relieved to be in a different location, away from all the flirtatious men. They had no respect for women. My new department heads, including my direct boss, would shower me with gifts and bring me lunch in appreciation of my hard work. One day the entire department, about thirty of us went to lunch, and they presented me with a Coach purse. They thanked me for being such a wonderful administrative assistant and how I go the extra mile to make sure deadlines were met. They assured me that I was doing a fabulous job and hopefully they were not expecting too much from me.

Chapter 28

FALLEN SKIES WAY

After seven years of marriage, I was beginning to fall out of love with Dale. I said to a friend one day, "I think Dale and I have the seven-year itch." It was a struggle to smile anymore. I did not want to share my bedroom with him anymore. We were fighting more than being civil with each other.

I was meeting up with friends more often after work. We would hang out and have a few drinks. I would sometimes invite Dale to happy hour if we were speaking to each other. One night Dale showed up at one of our after work socials uninvited. I was telling a joke to a few of my friends from work, and we were laughing uncontrollably and Dale thought we were laughing at him because apparently when he walked in all eyes were on him. He started knocking chairs over and throwing them across the room. "He's acting crazy" commented a friend of mine. I replied back "He must be drunk or high on drugs."

A few weeks later after dinner one night, my friend Ginny and I were chatting; the children were in bed, and I was waiting for Dale to pull into the driveway any minute when I received a phone call from the manager at the bar, saying Dale was passed out in the bushes. Ginny offered to get him. I accepted her offer since I was already in my PJs. Ginny told me the next day that Dale made a pass at her. He wanted to make love to her. I was devastated!

After knowing now I can't trust Dale even with my friends, especially if he is drinking, I began doubting our marriage. What I couldn't grasp was why Dale didn't want to come home after a hard day of working and relax and spend time with his family? I had full responsibility of taking the kids to daycare; picking them up after work and feeding and bathing them, while their dad was getting drunk at a bar.

A few weeks later, Dale came home one evening in an exceptionally nasty mood. "What's the matter with you? You've been here all night and the kids are still up. Where is my dinner?"

I replied, "Your dinner is in the refrigerator waiting for you."

He exploded, "In the refrigerator!" He walked over to the refrigerator and picked up his plate and threw it in the sink. Ugly and vicious words flew from our mouths without regard for little frightened ears and eyes. I ran to the living room, locking the door behind me. He began kicking the door and screaming at me. I finally opened the door, and he started swinging his arms at me and screaming at me for giving him a dirty look. Patrick and Nicole were begging their dad to stop fighting with me. The next day Nicole informed me that she wanted to go live with Maw maw (Dale's mother).

These types of situations became more and more frequent, and our anger and frustration kept building. In the past, up until a few months ago, I never confronted him with his anger issues. I guess you could say I was very timid so I cowered under his abusive authority. All I wanted was to be loved and accepted as his wife. God has created us to need love, acceptance, and freedom; these are part of our DNA, and we will never function well in life without them. My enthusiasm about life was again replaced with sadness and frustration due to not feeling loved by my husband.

My frustration came to a head when he arrived home one night, and I begged him for an explanation why he didn't call me to let me know he was going to be out so late. He started taking swings at me, throwing anything he could get his hands on, but I exploded and fought back. We were like two vicious pit bulls circling one another. I grabbed the mop and started swinging and hitting him. He managed to get the mop from me, and I ran to the knife drawer. I was furious. I started crying and fell to my knees and begged him to leave before he drove me insane. I wanted him out of the house, but he would not leave.

The next evening, I convinced him we needed time apart before we ended up killing each other. I wasn't sure that I could trust myself anymore. I also felt he wouldn't hesitate to harm me in one of his drunken rages. I packed a suitcase, and the kids and I stayed with Maw maw for a few months. After a few months away, Dale begged me to come home with the children. He apologized and said that he had quit drinking. Of course I forgave him. Dale did have my heart. I was so happy that he finally realized that drinking was not good for our marriage. He was a totally different person when he was drinking, an evil person.

That summer we did a lot of camping on the river and fishing with the children. We stayed busy every weekend; if not camping with the children, we were working in the yard or making improvements on our little farmhouse. We started going to church on Sundays. One Sunday afternoon we went for a Sunday drive after church. He turned to me and said, "Sharon, I am so sorry for all the heartache I have caused you the last several years. I really do want to be a good husband and father. I do agree with you that when I am drinking, I change into an evil person sometimes, and this is not healthy for our marriage." He continued, saying, "When I am drinking sometimes, I have blackouts because I don't remember everything. Things you tell me how I acted or things I say, I really don't believe I acted that way."

During our ride, I did not hear a sound from the back seat until we passed a playground and Nicole shouted, "Daddy, pull over, please; I want to swing." The kids jumped out and Dale opened the car door for me and hand-in-hand we walked toward the kids with smiling faces. We watched the children swing as we sat on the bench talking about the Sunday service. Dale wanted to know, "What is the Holy Spirit the pastor kept referring to?"

I tried to explain that the Holy Spirit is the supernatural spirit, Jesus (your teacher, counselor, and comforter). The pastor was explaining to us about when a husband and wife are submitting their life to Jesus, as their Lord and Savior, both will be living according to God's plan for marriage, and both will be open to the work of the Holy Spirit in their lives as individuals in their life together by receiving thoughts and ways of God. The Holy Spirit is the one who changes us to conform to the image of Jesus.

Dale then asked me, "How can I get that spirit?"

I replied, "You need to accept Jesus as Lord and Savior, and he will forgive all your sins. Then you will be saved and Jesus will live in your heart, referred to as the Holy Spirit and you will become Christ-like.

We tried to go to church every Sunday but it was getting less and less. Dale fell off the wagon and started hanging out at the bars again after work.

Maw maw was picking the kids up more and more from daycare due to my heavy work load at the office. I was supporting forty engineers since my promotion. I was also meeting up with friends from work for happy hour when it was convenient for me.

I missed my period one month and took a home pregnancy test. It was positive. Dale and I were both surprised at the test result. I cried and Dale made no comment when I told him. Diane was in the living room with Patrick and Nicole. At this time Patrick was nine and Nicole seven. I walked into the living room and announced to everyone that I had something special to share with them. "Patrick and Nicole, you are soon going to have a little brother or sister," I said with happy tears streaming down my cheeks.

Diane's remark was, "Sharon, how can you be pregnant when you and Dale don't even get along?" She continued to say, "It can't be Dale's!"

I ran upstairs to my bedroom and cried in my pillow. Why did she make that remark when she doesn't know what goes on behind our bedroom door. She was right; we did not have a loving relationship for the last six years, and she should have been encouraging her son to stop the drinking but she blamed me for the cause of our horrible marriage.

The next day I made an appointment with my doctor and was told I was about two months into the pregnancy. I was told by the doctor that he wanted me to have an amnio procedure done since I was almost thirty-seven years old. I scheduled the appointment and asked Dale if he would like to be there when the results of the gender came back. He agreed to take off work. We were told that the baby boy looked very healthy. The only concern was that he had a bigger head than normal.

Dale was so happy that he was going to have another son. We talked that night about selling the farmhouse and moving away from Boyds. We knew that we were going to need a fourth bedroom soon. We put our house up for sale the next day. The following day we had a contract on our home and were offered more than what we were asking. The future buyers had been interested in buying our house a year ago and stopped in one day and said to give them a call whenever we were interested in selling.

We moved to Laytonsville, my hometown, a few months later. We had bought a four-bedroom house on five acres with a built-in pool. Patrick and Nicole were very excited about their new home. They had many kids their age to play with in the new neighborhood. I was happy also but I knew down deep in my heart that Dale was not being faithful to me. He sometimes would not come home until 12:00, 1:00, or 2:00 in the morning. His excuse was that he was helping his friend, Jeff get his business up and running. He was opening a tanning salon in Poolesville.

One evening I approached Dale, saying politely, "May I remind you that the nursery needs to be furnished. When do you think we could go shopping for furniture?"

Dale responded, "We can't afford new furniture. You need to be looking in the paper for used." I finally found an ad for a changer and a dresser with a crib for only $300.00. It was in poor condition but after applying three coats of brown paint on the dresser and changer they looked almost new.

Early one Saturday morning, Dale walked into the kitchen where I was doing the breakfast dishes and said, "Goodbye" to me and the kids.

I reminded him, saying, "Melissa and Gary are coming for dinner."

He nodded his head and said he would try to be home by 6:00.

Melissa and Gary arrived at 7:00 and still no Dale. I tried many times calling him, but no answer. He missed dinner, and he didn't come home until the next evening. His excuse was that he and Jeff stayed drunk for a couple of days. I believed his story but felt very disappointed that he couldn't even give me a call. Again, a few days later he asked me for forgiveness, I agreed to forgive him.

I was now eight months pregnant and I was very tired of keeping up the house all by myself and caring for the kids. I would drop the Jared and Nicole off in Boyds Daycare every morning. Then I would drive to Rockville to work. I would need to be sitting at my desk by 8:00 a.m. I was exhausted by the end of the day, but I made the trip back to Boyds to the daycare and then on to Laytonsville. It was about a ninety-minute commute during rush hour.

One evening on my way home from Boyds, with Patrick and Nicole in the back seat, I was looking down at something on the seat beside me, and all of a sudden I heard and felt a loud bang. I had hit the car in front of me. My airbag deployed in my face. Apparently I accelerated because the airbag had startled me. I then caused a six car pile-up. Patrick and Nicole were crying. Minutes later I heard sirens.

The paramedics got the kids out of the car and put me on a stretcher. Patrick and Nicole were fine but Nicole was sobbing as they put us in the ambulance. I was worried about my baby inside my womb since I was not wearing my seat belt and I felt my stomach hit the steering wheel. The paramedics asked Patrick where his dad might be and Patrick said, "Maybe at work." It was 6:00 p.m., and I knew he probably was at a bar somewhere drinking with his bar friends.

We had been at the hospital for about two hours before Dale arrived. He walked over to me and asked, "Are you okay?"

I stared at him and said, "You are drunk! Why did you even bother coming?"

I would not allow him to take Patrick and Nicole home. I had Dale call his mother. She arrived and promised me she would take good care of them. I was told that I was having contractions so they said they wanted me to stay overnight. I was not released from the hospital until four days later. They were worried that I could possibly go into labor, and they also knew I was exhausted from the trauma to my body. Actually, I was on the verge of having a meltdown. I was so, so tired of doing and making sure everything was in order for our new baby.

Back at the office, I was informed that Amerisat was merging with General Communications and that I would have a longer commute to McLean, Virginia. They were offering some of the managers and directors a severance package. I also inquired about a severance package since I knew that I did not want to be commuting to Virginia every day. I was surprised when my boss told me that I would be getting a year's salary and that I also could draw unemployment.

Since the day I was called up to Walter's office I was always treated with the utmost respect and anything I wanted, I received. If it was coming in late, taking time off, they catered to all my needs. I received my severance package the next day. Jared arrived one week later.

Chapter 29

RUNNING SAND KNOLL

For the next year I enjoyed my new life at home with the children. I felt like a new person and I even started believing in myself again. Our family started attending Sunday Services at a Methodist Church in Laytonsville. Several months later Patrick, who was ten years old, Nicole, eight, and Jared, almost 1, were baptized since the minister talked me into having this done. I knew in my mind that it isn't until after you accept Jesus as your personal Savior that baptism follows because that is what I had been taught as a child. I felt honored that I was asked to teach the Nursery through K Sunday school class.

The children and I would make many trips to the beach the first summer I was home full time. Jared was so enjoyable to have in our lives. I actually started liking the sand when I saw how much pleasure it brought to my children.

Dale was still missing in action many evenings. He could not always account for where he was or with whom. Jeff and Dale were best friends now, and Jeff would stop by often to visit with Dale but never stayed long. One night when Jeff was visiting, he pulled up a chair next to me and said, "Hey, Sharon, I am having a cookout next Sunday and I would like to invite you, Dale and the kids."

I nodded and said, "Oh, how nice of you to include me and the children."

Sunday we arrived at Jeff's house. We were the first to arrive. A few minutes later, Jeff's mom and dad walked in, and Dale introduced me to theme. Later, Jeff's sister Dottie and her son walked in with a man behind her. Jeff introduced me to them. We sat around the table and made small talk. We had a couple of cocktails before dinner. The children were in the basement playing games with some of the other children. Jared was almost two years old, so he was keeping us on our toes running after him.

After dinner I helped Jeff's mom clean the dinner dishes. She asked me many questions about what my plans were now. "Do you plan on going back to work, or are you planning on staying home?" she asked. "Do you have a daycare for Jared yet if you do go back to work?" she inquired. I thought she was asking too many questions. I began looking around the house for Dale. I had not seen him for about an hour. Jared was getting tired, and I thought it was time to go. I went outside, walked around to the side of the house and saw Dale had Dottie next to the house speaking very quietly to her about something. I was surprised to see their faces turned white as snow. They had been caught! I suspected there was something going on between them, but I could not prove it until this moment. I turned and walked back into the house. I said my goodbyes and thanked Jeff for everything. I called for Patrick and Nicole.

It was a very quiet ride home. I had nothing to say to Dale. I knew I had to get my ducks in a row. The last nine years of my marriage to Dale had been mostly miserable, unhappy, and basically unhealthy for all of us, including the children. I stayed in the marriage because of the way I was raised; "Be forgiving and pray for a miracle," my mother would say. My dad would say to me, "God can change Dale." So I made a decision, despite the miserable existence that I had at home, to me it was easier to stay there than to move forward elsewhere because my parents were totally against me ending the marriage.

During my marriage with Dale, I had lost confidence in myself. I had no self-esteem. I let depression and apathy rule my life. The only thing that kept me motivated were my three wonderful children. I often thought about how I was failing my children since I was not raising them in a Christian home. Their precious little eyes saw so much anger, hatred, turmoil, physical abuse, and so much unhappiness.

What kept my life exciting for me was thinking someday I would have my own business, hopefully an interior design business. I thought about it every day, hoping that my dream someday would come true. I mentioned my dream to Dale one day and he informed me that I don't have the understanding or knowledge of running a business. Diane also commented, saying, "Sharon, you dream too much, which is a waste of time." I do agree with Diane that I dream too much, but I have always been a big dreamer and I knew in my mind that one day I will have my own interior design business.

A few days later, I saw in the paper that a Franchise Expo was scheduled for the first week in October at the Washington, D.C. Convention Center. I told Dale I planned on checking it out. He agreed to go with me. As we were walking up and down the aisles, I noticed a white van with a rainbow on the side with big letters "Decorating Den." A very attractive lady was standing by the van, and I asked her if she could give me some information on her franchise. I was very impressed with her, the van, and the company. I told her that I would be calling her in the near future.

In the days following my introduction to the Decorating Den franchise, I could only think about the rainbow on the van. I had finally found my rainbow and I knew in my heart and soul this rainbow was the light at the end of my tunnel. Dale and I had many discussions about me purchasing a Decorating Den franchise. He had many reservations about it working for me. He mentioned that there was no way we could have two successful businesses in the same household. Dale reminded me that I had three children to take care of. How can you run a design business when you do not have any interior design experience? He would have only negative things to say to me even though I knew I could make it work. I thought to myself, Dale and Diane have no idea who I am.

Despite all of their negative remarks about me having a business, it still could not suppress me. Nothing, nobody is standing in my way anymore.

I started reading self-help/motivational books. I became very determined to have my own business. I knew in my heart that this was God's plan. He had opened the right doors. I also knew in my heart that I would accomplish my dream and I would have a successful interior design business. I feel *yes, yes* in my future. I was ready to take charge of my life and my dream. I had $16,000 in my savings account, so I called Mary the next day and told her I wanted to meet with her. I was qualified after attending a few meetings. I thanked Mary for believing in me and showing me how to achieve my dream of having my own interior design business. I told Dale that I was moving forward with the franchising and asked him if I could borrow $9,000 so I could pay the $25,000 in full.

I was very impressed with the franchise since it is a national company with a great reputation. Each franchise is independently owned and operated. I was also impressed with Decorating Den's concept, "Your Decorating Den Interiors consultant can do the shopping for you, bringing merchandise, swatches, and samples to your home or office via the color van."

I signed a ten year contract with Decorating Den. It was maybe two months before I scheduled my first appointment. Dale in the meantime was pushing me to contact another franchise owner that he had met through me, saying, "Susan is going to go places because she is not timid; she is very driven so you need to follow in her footsteps if you are going to be successful and not lose the money that you have invested in this business." Honestly, I knew what I was doing. I wanted to be sure I knew everything before going on my first appointment. Once I had all my own techniques figured out (measuring, pricing, and ordering) I would be ready to soar; I am not a creeper.

The third month in business, I sold over $12,000.00. The first full year in business I was the number one franchise owner for our Washington, D.C., region.

The first year as an entrepreneur flew by very quickly. I kept Jared with me most days, and when Patrick and Nicole arrived home from their school day, I was there to greet them.

Dale did most of my window treatment installations, which was a big help financially because I did not have to pay an installer. One night we were on an installation, and the client did not like the way he hung the rod. She annoyed him with her nagging, and he dropped the rod and walked out. After that he told me I would have to find someone else.

I built my business up very quickly. I worked hard and used Decorating Den's support system. The director of my region said to me at one of our meetings that all the energy that I was putting into my business and the enthusiasm I kept expressing would take me to new levels in my life. Susan, the franchise owner who Dale thought was going to be very successful, lost her franchise within two years.

The first four years in business, I was one of the top forty franchises nationwide. I received many awards. I appeared on CBS "The Today Show" with Harry Smith. It was televised nationwide. I was asked to do a room makeover on a shoestring budget, showing it step by step. Decorating Den also designed a few rooms in one of Donald Trump's apartments in New York City and had a social hour with him at one of our visits.

I was also interviewed by ABC's, Channel 7 News, giving an overview of Decorating Den's one-stop shop design service. Due to the interview, I was hired by a couple of Channel 7 anchormen to help them with their homes in D.C. I also worked with a congressman and his wife at their home in Chevy Chase and also their vacation home in Connecticut.

One day I was sitting with a client on her newly constructed patio, discussing her future plans for decorating her recently renovated home. I said, "Wow, Shirley, who built your patio? It is absolutely stunning!"

She replied, "Sharon, I don't think you know him but his name is Adam Martin. He is a Mennonite and a really nice guy."

I almost passed out. I said, "Shirley, you might not believe me, but Adam is my dad."

She almost passed out!

She made a comment upon my departure, "Sharon, now I know why you are so kind and giving of your time and are gifted with a creative flair; it is because of your father. He has taught you well."

I thought to myself after leaving Shirley's house, what a small world, and I can't hide from my Mennonite upbringing. Shirley also could not believe I was raised in a Mennonite home. In my heart though I was so proud of my dad; he was very gifted and talented and a very kind man whom people loved. Some of his work was advertised in the *Architectural Digest* magazine. He received many awards for his outstanding designs of courtyards/walkways and waterfalls at some of the embassies in D.C.

After having many appointments with Shirley in redoing her window treatments, on my last visit with her she told me she was dying of stomach cancer. Her doctor informed her she might have only six months to live. She and I cried together. She shared with me her strong faith and that she was prepared for Heaven. She was raised Baptist and was a member of a Baptist Church. Our conversation was cut short when her son, Danny, walked in the door. Danny was their right-hand man in the family business. She did tell me in one of my visits that Danny was doing a fabulous job with the business, and she knew he was going to take the flower/plant business to the highest level possible and wished she could see it happen.

Danny was very driven. He worked 24-7 and did a lot of traveling for the family business. His dream was to have a jet, a multi-million dollar home on the bay, and, of course, a nice yacht someday. I was also very driven like Danny. At one of the Decorating Den's monthly sales meetings, I was told by the VP of marketing, "What you have accomplished in your first three years is an inspiration to many of us. How did you grow your business so quickly?"

I replied, "I put my flyers out religiously and once I get in the door, I know how to sell the product because I believe in having a beautiful home."

I often thought of my mother sharing her gift of selling with me at a very young age. Because of her encouraging words and her advice to me, I know what to say to the customer, and that has helped me in my Interior Design business. The most rewarding part of my business is making a new friend. I looked forward to meeting new people.

Dale became very bitter about me being away from home in the evenings. Eventually it took a toll on our relationship, and he gave me an ultimatum: is it our marriage or Decorating Den? I told him he was not being fair. This was my passion; I finally felt like I was making a difference in the lives of so many people. I knew I had a gift in designing, thanks to my dad. He was very creative and had many artistic abilities. Dale's mother was coming by the house every night after work. We had a schedule worked out that I would be home during the day with the children and after dinner I would get on the road and do my appointments and installations.

I did have a babysitter for Jared if I had to go to meetings or appointments during the day. One evening my installer and I had just left the house to do an installation when I received a phone call from Dale asking me if Jared was with me. I looked in the van and said, "No, why?"

Dale said, "Jared is nowhere to be found. He's not in the yard or the house."

I told Dale to check the sandbox because he loved to play in his sandbox. He would stay there most of the day. Dale replied, "No, that is the first place we checked." I became hysterical and pulled the van over. I went to the back of the van and opened the doors, and I did not see Jared.

I started yelling, "Oh my, where could Jared be?" I looked into the shelving units, and there he was, hiding behind some fabric books. He always would cry when I had to leave him in the evenings. He enjoyed being with me. I would always take him as much as possible with me. I scolded him for scaring us to death but I let him go with us that evening.

Dale and I continued having fights about me working all the time. I enjoyed working more than spending time with him. He was becoming a nitpicker about every little thing. I could do nothing right. He found fault in everything I did or said. He approached me one afternoon in the kitchen as I was enjoying my afternoon snack, a bowl of popcorn, saying "Sharon, have you completed your tax returns yet?"

I replied, "No, but I should have the returns completed and ready for you in a few days."

He walked toward me and yanked the bowl out of my hands and threw the full bowl of popcorn across the kitchen, hitting the floor with the popcorn flying everywhere. I stood there in disbelief asking him "Why did you just do that?"

He answered, "If you weren't running around with who knows who, it could have been done!" He walked out of the room; not even an apology was offered—or his help in cleaning up his mess.

He started drinking more, and was staying out more and more since he did not need to be home for the children, as his mother would stay with them until I finished my appointments. The marriage was headed for a breakup. I saw it coming when I had no desire to sleep with him anymore. I knew he was having an affair with Dottie. The drinking was destroying our marriage, and over the many years of living in turmoil, my pleasant, kind character changed to a very impatient, miserable character. When you are continually mistreated and abused, eventually you lose all your self-worth. I wanted to be the Sharon that I was many, many years ago, but I didn't have the energy to care about me. All my energy went to the children and my business.

One day I received a phone call from Sara, Danny's girlfriend, telling me that Shirley had succumbed to her stomach cancer. I attended the wake. At the funeral home, Danny asked me if I could help him and Sara with their decorating needs for their new home. I told them I would be happy to work with them.

The following week I decided that my marriage wasn't worth fighting for. I was beginning to hate Dale, and I hated the way he made me feel: so unappreciated and worthless. I admired Danny and Sara's relationship; they were like best friends. I did not have that with Dale; actually we despised each other. Every day was a struggle to get out of bed. I just wanted to sleep, so I didn't have to deal with my sadness. I often thought about seeking professional counseling for my depression, but I knew that until Dale quit drinking and staying out late at night, the counseling was not going to make a difference.

I began sleeping in Nicole's bed. I picked up Patrick from school one day, and on the way home I mentioned to Patrick that I was thinking about leaving his dad. Dale had wanted me to give up my business, and I could not walk away from something that I totally believed in. Patrick asked me, "Mom, what about me and Nicole?" I replied, "Patrick, I want to take you and Nicole with me."

Fourteen years is a long time to be in a marriage when you don't feel good about your partner. One day after a really bad confrontation with Dale, he ripped the outfit I had on that day in shreds. I told him I wanted a divorce. He came over to me and started choking me when Patrick came to my rescue, and Dale released his grip on my neck. Dale was very apologetic to us and walked out in tears.

I came home the next day after my appointments, and Dale had sent me an arrangement of beautiful red tulips. The note read, "I am so sorry for all the pain I have caused you, and I hope you can forgive me for hurting you." In my mind it was too late. I had lost all my love for him. There was no more forgiveness; I was finished! The last straw was when I caught him with Dottie on the side of her brother's house engrossed in a deep conversation. I knew something was not right. I could read people well, and Dottie never had much to say to me. She would always keep her distance. She was not friendly to me.

Dale continued sending me flowers every day for two weeks. Our home looked like a funeral parlor. With every floral arrangement was a note saying how much he loved me and did not want me to leave. He told me if I stayed, he would seek counseling. I knew I could never trust him again! He was so deceitful and had been all of my years with him. He really did not know how to be faithful and truly love me.

I confided with my parents about my troubling marriage and how abusive Dale was to me, mentally and physically. I told them about him being involved with another woman. I also told them I planned on leaving Dale as soon as I found a house to rent. My parents reminded me that when I took my marriage vow before God that I vowed to be his wife until we were departed by death. My dad reminded me that our marriage vows were made "in the name of God." He continued, saying, "Sharon, if you leave Dale, you know you will never be free in God's eyes to ever remarry. If you do, your soul will go directly to hell."

I reflected back on my wedding day and the ceremony as I was repeating the vow after the pastor, "In the name of God, I, Sharon, take you Dale to be my husband, to have and to hold from this day forward for better, for worse, for richer, for poorer, in sickness and in health, to love, honor, and cherish, until we are parted by death. This is my solemn vow." I glanced at my parents sitting in the pews to the right, and my dad was looking up at the ceiling with tears streaming down his face. My mother was also crying. I was thinking to myself, are they happy tears or sad tears?

I confirmed with Dale that I would be moving out within a week. Patrick and Nicole decided to live with their dad. Dale did tell me that I could not take them with me. My heart was broken again to know I would be leaving them behind. We did agree I could see them anytime during the week, and they would stay with me every other weekend.

I was extremely sad about leaving Patrick and Nicole. I was on the verge of reconsidering the separation since I knew what the Bible teaches about leaving a marriage, especially when children are involved. My heart was telling me to stay, but my mind was telling me the marriage was over. I had lost all love for Dale; actually I had so much anger built up toward him. I was tired of him trying to control me. He expected me to abide by his rules only. I was packing my belongings one morning, when I heard a knock at the door. Dale was still at home in his office and he yelled upstairs, "Sharon, your brother, Steve, wants to talk to you!"

I yelled back, "I'll be down in a few minutes."

As I approached Steve, he had his Bible opened and was reading a verse from the Bible to Dale. Dale threw his hands up and said, "Steve, it's not me ending the marriage, it is Sharon, so you need to preach to her."

Steve turned to me and said, "Sharon, please take time to think about what you are doing to your children. Pray to God who loves you so much and wants you to save your marriage. You need to forgive Dale for all his wrong doings, and God will restore your marriage. Sharon, you know God can heal your heart. He can give you the fulfillment and happiness you are seeking. You do not need to find it in another relationship." Apparently someone had been spreading news about me being involved with another man. I told him I was leaving and no one was going to change my thinking. My marriage was over and had been over for a long time. I was tired of feeling worthless and was tired of sharing my husband with another woman or maybe women! I was ready to move on and that was the final say in that matter.

Dale did help me with the move into my new home. We settled everything out of court and pretty much agreed on most things. We were very accommodating to each other's desires on what each wanted. I was so sad though not being able to take all my children with me. I knew in my heart and soul that I was making the biggest mistake by allowing Patrick and Nicole to live with their father.

Chapter 30

HIGH TIDE PATH

*W*hat's next? I was now a single parent and a hard-working entrepreneur whose desire was to become a very successful independent woman.

After I left Dale, I worked even harder and longer hours. I helped with many home shows at the fairgrounds and convention centers whenever possible. I would have many workshops at community centers and libraries. Even when I had time to spare, which I should have been spending with family, I would deliver flyers, sometimes thousands in a span of a month. I was determined to show the people who didn't think I could survive on my interior design business that they were wrong.

In keeping with my lifestyle I was still having fun, and I continued to put my business first and foremost in my life. I continued being on the top forty list of franchise owners. I won a trip to Cancun. I was presented a check for $9,000.00 at one of the conferences because I was one of the top three franchise owners who had the most points by using our approved suppliers. I was having fun competing and being one of the best in sales! It was very motivating to be recognized as one of the best. It brought back happy memories when my mom praised me about being the best salesperson when I was selling cards for her.

Throughout the next year, while I was living life to its fullest; working hard and playing hard, I took a dive into a relationship with a very kind man who always had great things to say about me. He would build me up so much that I actually thought I was the best, and I had what it takes to be very successful. He would tell me how honest I was; how beautiful I was inside and out. I actually started believing in myself again. I had met Vic at one of our home shows about a year before. I was still married, but I liked having him around because he was so nice to me. He had shown me his portfolio at one of the shows, and I was very impressed with his work. His profession was making custom rugs. He and I would meet for lunch whenever I had time and just talk about the interior design business and my plans for the future.

I confided in Vic that I wanted to franchise my own interior design business someday, taking it worldwide. I was always a big dreamer. I remember as a small child I wanted to take my love for God and Jesus worldwide. Everything I wanted to accomplish in life was to take it worldwide. I was always very excited about reaching for the stars and making life exciting for all the people in my life. I wanted the best for everyone. I really had a desire to make a difference for the better in people's lives.

Vic was my biggest cheerleader saying always to me, "Sharon, you have a very special gift. You are a great designer. People love you and you love people. You show so much enthusiasm in everything you do. You are the best salesperson I have ever known." His words were always so uplifting.

Our relationship became more serious than what I wanted. What I really needed was to have a relationship with God again, not another man. This is not what I had envisioned so soon, being crazy in love. I was becoming obsessed and very crazy for his love and attention. He had spoiled me with his kindness and love for me. I eventually confided in Vic about me being raised Mennonite and how devastated my parents were about me leaving Dale. I knew in my heart my parents' deepest desire was that I would discover the grace of God and start living a clean, godly life and go back to Dale. Their hearts were grieving knowing that my decision was final.

One early morning as I was leaving to take Jared to school, a sheriff pulled into my driveway and jumped out saying, "Are you Sharon?"

I said, "Yes what is it, are my children okay?"

He replied, "Yes, your children are okay but your husband is not; he wants a divorce!" I stood on the steps confused; I could not believe he had filed for a divorce so soon.

I became really involved with Vic after the divorce papers were served. I would see him as much as possible. He would spend a lot of time at my place entertaining Jared when I had office work to do. I was burning the midnight oil at both ends; working at my business and working on my relationship with Vic. When Vic finally realized how serious I was becoming, he started backing off. He would go sometimes a whole week without making plans with me. I was extremely hurt by his actions: not returning my phone calls or turning me down for a date. I was missing him so much.

I invited him to my cousin's house for a birthday celebration, and I was surprised that he accepted. We had a wonderful time; I saw many friends I had not seen in awhile and after a few drinks, I became very outgoing and friendly, which did not go over very well with Vic. He approached me and said he was ready to leave. I found Jared, and we were on our way home with Vic driving since he said I had too many drinks. After he pulled into my driveway, he called a cab to pick him up. I pleaded with him to stay but he said, "No. You need to take Jared inside and go to bed."

After the cab picked him up, I was completely heartbroken and upset. I did not want him to leave. I couldn't understand why he was becoming so distant. What is wrong with me? I was feeling rejected and I did not like this feeling. I told Jared to come with me. We were going to Vic's. Jared at this time was five years old. When I arrived at Vic's, I did not see any lights on, but I rang the doorbell. I knew he was home because his car was in the driveway. I rang the bell again, and again, but no answer. I walked around the house with Jared and saw in the basement window that he was lying in bed talking on the phone. I started knocking on the casement window, but he completely ignored my knocks.

I yelled "Vic, if you do not answer the front door and talk to me, I will be coming in through this window!"

He did not move. I stood there with Jared by my side and said, "Jared, I am going to knock this window out, and I am going to jump in. Then I want you to jump in after me. I will catch you!" That is what we did! After I was in Vic's house, standing next to his bed, he looked at me like I was crazy! Yes, I was crazy in love, and I could not understand why he could not explain to me why he was keeping his distance. After all, I had spent many hours and money providing him window treatments for his house.

He jumped up out of bed and said, "I don't believe what you just did! You entered my house without my permission. I could have you arrested, do you know that?"

I started crying and Jared started crying. Vic walked us up the stairs to his living room and said, "Sharon, you need to leave now; it is over with us."

I became very angry now and started ripping down his window treatments that I had provided for him.

He calmed me down and said, "Sharon, I can't believe you drove here with Jared in the car."

I replied, "Vic I am fine to drive; I am angry because I deserve an explanation why you do not want to spend time with me like you used to."

He assured me that tomorrow we will talk about our relationship. He called me the next day and invited me to dinner. I called my niece, Christy, asking her if she could watch Jared for a few hours.

I was looking forward to having a quiet evening with Vic. Actually, it did not go the way I thought it would. He gave me devastating news about an illness he has known about since a young boy. He mentioned that he probably would not live to see fifty. Vic is thirty-eight years old. He went on to say that he and all of his siblings, except for one brother, have this kidney disease, which is incurable and hereditary. Most people live to be about forty years old if they aren't lucky enough to have a kidney transplant. Vic had tears in his eyes as he told me of losing a brother a few years ago (he was only twenty-seven years old); his only sister (thirty-years old) is very sick and is dying, and another brother is on dialysis four times a week and is very ill.

I had tears in my eyes when I responded to him, "Vic, why didn't you tell me earlier on about this? Why didn't you share this with me sooner? I feel so ashamed of my actions these last few weeks."

He spoke softly, "Sharon, I don't like talking or thinking about my illness."

I thought back to the days when he would not show up on the job, and I would not get a phone call telling me that he was not going to be able to keep the appointment; it was because he was a sick man and a very depressed man.

Vic had known since he was sixteen years old that his life was going to be short lived. How sad for him and his siblings to live with this thought every day. I apologized to Vic for all my horrible actions and picked up the check for dinner. We decided that night we would continue to be friends only, with no benefits. He wanted it that way, and he said to me that I should go back to Dale because there will be no other man to care or love my children like their father.

Vic continued saying, "Sharon, I really don't think you will ever find a man that would want a relationship with you, knowing you have children.

My thoughts turned to Richard who welcomed Kelly (Kimberly's daughter) into his life as his own daughter, and I saw firsthand, that he had as much love in his heart for her as if she was his biological daughter. Richard was different though than most men; he had integrity and respect and was a very kind man.

Vic and I continued to stay in touch. He continued doing custom rugs for my clients, and he would drop by to play with Jared on occasion. He loved spending time with Jared. He would take Jared to the pool and to the park when I was busy with office work.

One night as I was on my way home from an appointment, I received a telephone call from Richard saying he and Kimberly (his second wife) were planning on separating after eleven years of marriage. I had not seen or talked with my brother in over eight years since Dale and Richard's Home Improvement business went under. Richard and Dale became very bitter toward each other, and I had lost all contact with my brother and his family.

I said, "Richard, I am so sorry. Is there anything I can do for you?"

He answered back, "Yes, do you have a room for me?"

Richard moved in a few days later. Richard had two children (David and Christy) with Carol (his first wife) with whom I have stayed in contact with, but I had not seen his two daughters (Jennifer and Emma) with his second wife (Kimberly) and his adopted daughter, Kelly, in eight years.

After Richard's divorce with his first wife Carol, my parents never saw Richard again. It was Richard's choice to have nothing to do with Mom and Dad because they informed him that he could visit with his children but not with his second wife. They do not condone divorce and with their belief in remarrying, which is a sin in their mind, Kimberly would never be welcomed at their home. This was one of the Mennonite's restrictions. My brother decided to cut all ties with the family. I did have contact with my brother and Kimberly the first two years of their marriage.

I was very excited that my children would finally know their cousins. Every other weekend, Richard's girls would visit, along with Patrick and Nicole. I always looked forward to the weekend that all the children were with me. I would try not to go on appointments so I could spend quality time with them. Many Saturdays when I had all the children, I would pile them and the neighbor children in my Decorating Den van and drop them off in twos to deliver flyers in neighborhoods throughout my assigned territory. They would have a blast laughing and singing as they rode in the back of my van. I always gave them each a few dollars and after a few hours of delivering flyers, we would have lunch at Jerry's Pizza.

One weekend I decided to take all the children to Harrisonburg, Virginia for a Mennonite family reunion. Jennifer and Emma were so overwhelmed with their Mennonite relatives. The visit did not go as well as I would have liked, but at least my mother and father finally got to meet Jennifer and Emma. After that visit, they would never see each other again.

That night while lying in bed and thinking about the Mennonite beliefs and all their restrictions, I was beginning to have many bad thoughts about the Mennonite way (at least my parents' Mennonite conference). The Mennonite religion had torn our family apart. Where is the unconditional love my parents talked about when I was a young child? They were not showing me forgiveness in their heart toward my brother. Just because Richard had sinned, why do they think if they condone his second marriage it would keep them out of heaven? I was so confused how my parents could allow religion to separate them from their children. My parents had always showed so much love toward me and my siblings when we were younger. I am having a very hard time accepting all their new changes and beliefs.

About fifteen years after Uncle Mahlon died from the car accident, I attended my aunt's second wedding, which was at a Mennonite Church, and the pastor of this more liberal Mennonite church (not my home church) approached me saying, "Sharon, I think about you often regarding the way you were treated on that horrible communion Sunday, and I just want you to know how sorry I am for you and your family. I want you to know that a lot of the members of the Lancaster Mennonite conference did not agree with the Bishop's actions toward you; it was totally wrong." I saw tears in his eyes, and he continued saying, "Sharon I hope you have forgiven the Bishop."

I replied, "I have forgiven, but I cannot forget. I will hurt over this for a lifetime I am sure because I have also lost my once-so-wonderful parents."

The pastor replied, "Sharon I need to tell you something in confidence, a member of your family was involved with the decision not to serve you communion and that family member told the Bishop if he served you communion, he and his family were taking their membership elsewhere."

I was dumbfounded; I didn't know how to respond. Actually, I did not want to know who that family member was that destroyed my relationship with my parents and God because I was afraid of what I might do or say. Since that horrible day, I have been living my life without God's grace, love, and wisdom and without my parents'

Christian guidance. My mind could not understand how a Christian family member could do so much harm to a child of God, and destroy a very loving family. I remember as a child I was taught in church that it is biblical to always show compassion by doing good to all even if he/she is involved in sin. Galatians 6:1 says, "Brothers, if someone is caught in a sin, you who are spiritual should restore him gently." The only person who showed me compassion that Sunday morning was Jeanette Goodman.

Apparently, my being denied communion put a big strain on my parents' relationship with the church and the family member who was behind the decision not to serve me communion. My family member should have shown humility, love, and genuine empathy and sensitive support to my parents and me, but instead it was harsh treatment and condemnation which led to losing three souls, Richard, Ann Marie, and mine.

My parents had allowed the Mennonite church to dictate how they accept and love their lost children. The Mennonite conference my parents belong to now has even more restrictions on their members. I remember about nine years ago, Mom called me, crying about missing Richard and her grandchildren, David and Christy, due to losing all contact with him. She did say that she had stopped by to visit with David and Christy, but they did not answer the door. She was heartbroken. I would send pictures of Richard's children to her.

Mom was very sad about hurting Richard for not accepting Kimberly as his wife. Mom and dad would say to me, "We do not want to miss Heaven." In their mind and the church rules, they believed if they welcomed his second wife into their home, they would be considered failures and God would punish them by sending them to hell.

I was spending a lot of my free weekends with Danny and Sara. I had been decorating their home for almost a year now. Their house was huge with a gorgeous patio and pool. Danny used my dad and brothers to construct his patio. Danny was very impressed with their work. Sara mentioned to me one day when I was visiting with her, "Hey, Sharon, I finally met your Mennonite brothers. They are really nice. Your brothers are very quiet and reserved, unlike you!"

I replied, "Those are just a few of the characteristics of being a Mennonite.

Danny and Sara were crazy and a lot of fun! They invited me to an outing one night in Baltimore at the Inner Harbor, and I had a fabulous evening hanging out with their friends. After that night, they were my party partners. My heart is into the club life now and all the fun that comes with it. Within a few months I became involved with another man. I was out with Sara one night, and we stopped by a club to have a drink. As we were leaving, a nice-looking man approached me asking me if I was married.

I replied, "No" and I asked him, "Are you married?"

I did not have much trust in men these days. We exchanged phone numbers and he followed me to the door, asking me what I was doing later. I said nothing so we hooked up later that night just talking the night away until the early morning. I was very attracted to him. He was very nice. He listened. He sympathized. I thought to myself I have finally found a good man.

Chapter 31

CRADLEROCK WAY

*I*t had been two years since I left Dale, and I was ready for a relationship again. Tommy was also very impressed with me being an entrepreneur and my work ethic. He often commented to me, "Sharon, you are a very hard worker."

Tommy would spend his money on me and lavish me with so much attention, which I was not used to. He was almost eight years older than me. This relationship was moving seriously fast. We were two lonely hearts searching for love. We were a couple committed to each other after spending the weekend together. We could not get enough of each other.

Richard also met another woman, Michelle, and was planning on marrying her in the near future. He moved out, but I continued seeing Jennifer and Emma whenever possible. I enjoyed having my nieces around. Christy, Richard's first daughter with Carol, watched Jared whenever I needed her to help out.

I was beginning to have financial struggles because I was paying all the bills alone with no husband or anyone to help me. I was struggling because I was still keeping my lifestyle as when I was married. I continued going to the malls, buying whatever I wanted. I would go out to dinner with the children or friends almost every night if I did not have an appointment. I was getting behind with my suppliers and my monthly bills. I began using my credit cards to pay bills. I eventually reached my limit on all of them. I was behind one month on my rent and I was becoming very scared for Jared and me.

I called my dad and asked if he had $10,000 that I could borrow, and his reply was, "Sharon, I warned you about possible hardships and that you should be putting money away for a rainy day."

I said, "Dad, can you help me out?"

His reply, "I am so sorry Sharon, but I do not have $10,000.00."

I confided in Tommy that I was having financial difficulties, and he asked me if I would consider moving in with him to help with the financial burden. He added, "Sharon, I have been looking for you all of my life, and I promise you I will take good care of you and Jared from this day forward. Sharon, I want to grow old with you. I have finally found true love, you. I am ready to offer you my home, my heart, and the rest of my life." I told him I would have to think about his offer. I knew in my heart I was ready for someone to fill the empty void in my crazy life. A few months later I called Mom and told her I would like to come and talk to her about something very important and she said, "Sharon, you sound worried about something, what is wrong?" I told her I would like to tell her in person.

When I arrived at my parents' home, somewhat troubled about what I was going to tell them, thoughts were running through my head about my troubled life, and I knew down in the depth of my soul that what I was about to tell my parents would put them over the edge with me. After I told them I had moved in with my boyfriend, Mom began crying. Still crying she said, "Sharon, you need to go back to Dale since he is your husband in God's eyes. Sharon, you are not the girl I raised. I am very disappointed with you and all the bad and sinful choices you are making. Your life is headed for destruction, and I hope I am not alive to see it happen!"

So little does my mom know about the life I am now living; I am a free-spirited woman with a lot of excitement in my life. I would entertain my friends by being the center of attention at parties. We would have boob flashing contests with the men judging. Our nights of partying consisted of drinking and doing shots until we were almost passed out. My friends, Sara and Danny, were often having pool parties or inviting me out to nightclubs.

My business never stopped me from having fun. I played very hard. I would rent limos for special occasions. I was celebrating my forty-third birthday with my girlfriends. Barbie and Darla, my Decorating Den friends were in charge of our night out on the town (Washington, D.C). We had coolers full of the best wine and champagne. On all of our club stops, Barbie (my friend with a big smile and big flirtatious sky-blue eyes knew how to soften the bouncer's authority with her sexy and lean model physique) made known to the bouncers that it was my birthday, and she made sure that I was treated like a "queen." There was no waiting in a line to get in and once in, we never had to wait long for a drink. I had nice-looking guys asking me to dance, thanks to Barbie (I think maybe she told them I wanted to dance with them) or maybe it was Sara's beauty that was attracting all the handsome guys. I was enjoying the moment to the fullest. I was on a mission to have a blast with my girlfriends. We danced the night away with so much talking and laughing.

After a few more getaways, from celebrations of milestone birthdays to divorce parties with my girlfriends over the next few years, my relationship with Tommy was becoming a nightmare. He was beginning to accuse me of having an affair. He was checking my office voice mail messages often. On occasion I caught him following me when I was going on appointments. He did not trust me. One night I came home from an appointment, and he had locked the dead bolt for which I did not have a key. I was devastated to think I might not have a home. I called him and an hour later he arrived home. I was in tears sitting in my car and wondering if he was going to let me stay. When he saw that I had been crying, I think he felt sorry for me. He didn't like to see me upset. He gave me a big hug and said he was sorry.

Tommy attended the Decorating Den Conference in Reno, Nevada, with me several months later in May. I received several awards at the conference, and he was so proud of me. I also received the President's Club Award, which is one of the best awards. I did remind him of his accusations of me having an affair and how can that be possible when I am selling $300-400 thousand a year?

We had a wonderful time in Nevada, taking in all the sightseeing possible. We drove to Lake Tahoe and spent a day on the lake; how breathtaking the snowcapped mountains that surrounded us were on the crystal blue lake, on a beautiful sun-filled, spring day.

That glorious day sitting on a bench overlooking the lake, I thanked God for all His blessings and for giving me the opportunity to soar high with my interior design business. I also thanked Him for directing me to the best franchise ever, Decorating Den Interiors. My life finally seemed fulfilled; I am a successful businesswoman, thanks to the best family, the Bugg family, owners of Decorating Den Interiors. When I arrived home from the conference, I had a message from Mom asking me to call her. I called her the next day, and she begged me to come see her. She told me that she was not well. I promised her I would visit soon.

Four months later, I received a phone call at 5:30 a.m. on a Saturday from my brother telling me that Mom had passed away. I never did get to visit with her. What happened next is so unbelievable; I smelled an aroma of peppermint paddy candy which my mom enjoyed making for the family.

I asked Tommy lying next to me, "Tommy, are you chewing peppermint gum?"

He asked me, "Why?" and he said, "I don't smell peppermint."

I cried and cried knowing it was my mother's spirit saying goodbye to me.

A few weeks after my mother's death, Tommy and I decided to go out for a drink. We met some friends at a local restaurant and did not have just one drink but a few too many. It was getting late. We had closed the restaurant down. On our way home, Tommy lost control of his rental car and hit a ditch, then a few mailboxes, and a concrete embankment. He managed to get the car back on the road and continued driving the car with blown-out tires. I knew we were lucky he did not hit the huge tree that I saw coming at us.

As we reached our street he pulled into the parking lot across from his house. He turned to me and said, "Run as fast as you can to the house." We just got in and I was preparing a snack, since we didn't have dinner, when I heard the doorbell ring. Tommy informed me not to answer the door. I saw him crashing to the floor. The doorbell rang again and again. I then heard a man's voice shouting, "Police, let us in or we are coming in on our own!" I was very scared at this point so I opened the door.

Two policemen were standing in front of me. They looked very disgusted and angrily said to me, "Who was driving the car that left the scene of an accident?"

I did not reply soon enough as they pushed by me and saw Tommy lying on the floor. They started kicking him and shaking him but he did not respond to their abusive touches. They began walking through the house asking me why all the cabinet doors were open and I told them I was preparing a snack. They began drilling me for answers about our night out. They wanted to know how much we had to drink; where we were drinking and they continued saying that they could not believe we continued driving the totaled car. How in the world did they already know what damage was done; apparently they have also seen the car. We had only been home about fifteen minutes.

When the policemen left I went to bed sobbing, thinking about my mother and her last words to me during our last visit together. "Your life without God is headed for destruction, and I hope I am not alive to see this happen." I was beginning to see what my mother meant by that statement. Thank God he spared my life again since I thought the big tree coming at me was going to take my life.

The next morning Tommy called the car rental agency and reported the accident. The charges against us were truly becoming a nightmare in the days to follow. The car had been totaled and the police report was three pages long. There were consequences to be paid which did take a toll on my relationship with Tommy.

I remember going to a Billy Graham's crusade as a young adult, and he brought up the drinking issue that so many people live with. Leave it alone; drinking is the cause for so much evil in this world, he would always preach. He would stress, "What people need is Jesus Christ as their Lord and Savior. When you receive Christ as Lord and Savior, He will make us over in a twinkling of an eye and the changes will be forever. The drinking will only drown your troubles temporarily and the consequences of drinking can be devastating to you and others." When Billy Graham extended us an invitation to receive Jesus in our hearts, or rededicate our life to Jesus, Kimberly my sister-in-law walked to the altar, rededicating her life to Jesus. I was not ready yet to commit my life to Jesus. I was still very angry with God. I felt God had deserted me, and I was also questioning Jesus' love for me; and I was not ready to totally give up the partying life.

Reflecting back on my life, living on the wild side, the drinking was the cause of my miserable existence. Drinking was the cause of the breakup of my marriage; the many hangovers which caused the waste of a whole day by staying in bed; flashing boobs; saying and doing stupid things. Drinking is the cause of so many deaths! There were many nights as a teenager and a young adult I was behind the wheel, and the next morning I didn't even remember driving home. How stupid and immature getting drunk is!

A few years ago I met a wonderful lady by the name of Marcie, a friend of my friend Kim, and she confided in me the tragic news that her daughter would be spending many years in jail for hitting and killing a young girl crossing a street in Ocean City, Maryland. She continued telling me that she only had two drinks but was charged with manslaughter and was sued by the deceased girl's parents. Marcie and her husband lost their home and all their lifetime savings due to their daughter being under the drinking age. Marcie was in tears as she shared her story with me. She said her daughter attended Lancaster Mennonite High School because she heard LMHS had so much integrity and had some of the best Christian teachers on the East Coast.

Marcie added, "My daughter was so driven to succeed in life. She also loved the Lord and strived to live Christ-like every day. She wanted to become an international lawyer someday in the Third

World Countries, helping the less fortunate, but now her dream has been shattered forever."

"Marcie, "I said with so much tenderness, "I am so, so sorry for all your pain and heartache, but you know God knows what is in your daughter's heart and soul and He knows how special she is to you and I will bet you a million dollars she will not spend many years in jail." I asked Marcie "Are you or any of your family Mennonites?"

"No," Marcie replied.

I said, "Well, I was just curious because she attended a Mennonite High School, and it is very unusual for children to attend if not a Mennonite." I added, "I was a Mennonite many years ago and attended the Lancaster Mennonite High School."

Marcie's mouth dropped wide open, saying "You were a Mennonite?"

"Yes and a very devout Mennonite until I was seventeen years old!"

I thanked God that night after having dinner with my friends and Marcie, for keeping me safe and free of causing my parents more grief from all the devastating consequences that drinking can do to a person and a family. I also said a prayer for Marcie and her daughter that God would comfort them through this horrific ordeal and that something great would come out of this terrible nightmare.

My relationship with Tommy was headed for disaster. I became pregnant about six months later. I was forty-seven years old and could not believe it. Tommy could not believe it either and said there was no way he was the father of this baby since he is sterile and has been shooting blanks for many years. It was so hurtful that he was accusing me of messing around since I truly loved him with all my heart and soul. I was devastated by his remark of not being faithful to him. I could not keep back the tears. I cried myself to sleep that night.

I once again went through the abortion counseling process. They told me that due to my age, I should consider an abortion as soon as possible. The night before the scheduled abortion, Tommy informed me he would take me and I accepted his offer. I was very tired so

I retired early to bed. During the night I was awakened by the bed shaking. I thought Tommy was having a seizure but when my eyes became focused on him, he was masturbating while watching a porn flick on TV. I yelled, "You are disgusting!" I jumped out of bed and left the room commenting to him that he was a sick little puppy.

The next morning I was up early and out of the house. Tommy was still sleeping; probably hung over from all the drinks he was inhaling the night before. I drove myself to the clinic. I cried out to God. "Dear God, I know this is wrong. Please stop me if you don't want me to go through with this even if you have to take my life."

In my heart I really meant that request I just made to God. I was ready again to give up on life. The person that I really loved again has ruined my trust and love for him.

As I was waiting for my name to be called, I started thinking about my mother's life and how she was such an inspiration to me as a young child and teenager. My childhood memories of her were so precious. She was so sweet and loving to me, my siblings, and especially to my dad. Oh how I wished she was still living. Reflecting back on my life as a young teenager, I remembered how she would encourage me to have the same personality qualities as she and Dad: compassion, gentleness, love for others, and love for God. I cherished her memory and how I do so, so miss her.

After the procedure was over, I lay in the recovery room crying my heart out about what I had just done. The nurse came over to me and started wiping my tears away with a roll of paper towels. She said, "Sharon, there was a guy here earlier, banging on the door asking for you, but we turned him away since you said nothing to us about a man possibly joining you."

I softly replied, "Yes, you did the right thing by not letting him in." In my mind I was thinking the only reason why he was there, most likely, was to make sure I did go through with the procedure. I did not want to go home, but I knew in my mind it was just going to be temporary.

Chapter 32

TOPSY-TURVY PATH

*A*nother year had gone by, and I was still living with Tommy. My interior design business was booming, and my sales were almost a half million for the year. I had extra cash to have some cosmetic surgery done. I made an appointment to inquire about having liposuction done to my outer and inner thighs. I thought my legs were too big and unattractive. After consulting with my plastic surgeon, it was a go. I scheduled the surgery, and he informed me that the recovery time would be about five days.

After the surgery, I was in excruciating pain. In the recovery room a nurse approached me and gave me instructions on what I needed to do. The nurse pulled the sheet down to explain the function of the girdle that I was now wearing. (The girdle was from above my waist to below the knees with an opening at the bottom/ vaginal area). She mentioned I should take only bird baths. No showers, until the doctor says it is okay, probably about two weeks.

After the second day of recovering, the pain was getting worse; I was on very strong pain killers, which did not seem to be working. I wanted to die; the pain was worst than having a baby. Jared was very attentive to me and would wait on me throughout the day and sat by my side as much as possible. He was very worried and scared for me because I cried a lot and was constantly throwing up.

After my follow-up visit with the surgeon five days later; he informed me that I would be able to take the girdle off in five days to shower. The day I took the girdle off and saw my legs, I screamed and thought I was going to pass out. They were disgusting—black and blue and swollen three times the size they were before the surgery. During my shower I cried the entire time, thinking how vain I was becoming about my body. I wanted perfection; I was not happy with my body at all.

During the recovery time I was bored out of my mind so I thought about continuing writing about my life experiences. About twenty years ago I had started writing my story about being raised in a missionary home as a Mennonite but with children and working full-time I had to put it on the back burner.

Reflecting back on my life now, I am almost forty-nine years old, and I have totally a different outlook where I want to go with my story. Wanting to blame the Mennonites and my parents for my lifelong struggles, due to being rejected by the Church, is not what I want to do. I want my story to possibly help other women who have the same struggles as I have had and are in destructive relationships. I want to inspire women to not make the same mistakes as I have. Never lose God in your life. With all that life offers you, you need to keep God in your life and choose your friends wisely and make the right choices. Without God, you will be a very unhappy soul, living in poverty.

My mother was right, saying, "If you don't have Jesus in your life, you will be the most miserable creature living in poverty." I remember my dad often saying our real poverty is lack of faith, lack of honor, lack of respect for each other, and the lack of love and affection for all men of goodwill.

My father always reminded me when I conversed with him on the telephone that my life could be very fulfilling if I lived for the Lord instead of Satan. I truly did understand that I had forsaken the God of my youth. God has made us in a way that until we return to his arms, we will be like the prodigal son, a miserable and misplaced creature in the world. I was beginning to feel miserable about my life.

Finally, after three weeks of recovery, I resumed going on appointments and installations. The first appointment after my surgery was helping my installer deliver a sofa to a client. As I was helping to carry the sofa from the van to the house, I felt wetness between my legs, and I am thinking to myself, what is going on down there; I have a tampon in (that time of the month). I could not wear panties yet because I was still wearing my girdle with the openings for doing your business. I found a bathroom and checked my legs, and sure enough there was blood running down inside my legs, and the tampon was gone. I frantically ran through the house and went outside where I saw my client's dog with my tampon in her mouth running toward the house. I was chasing after her, hoping to get it from the dog before my client saw it dangling from her teeth.

It was too late. My client was saying, "Bella, what do you have in your mouth. Come here little Bella, what is it?" I almost fainted when she pulled it out of Bella's mouth and said, "Bella where did you get this?"

I stood there with my mouth hanging wide open and said, "I saw her pick it up from outside."

My client said, "Oh, maybe she got it out of the trash; it is trash day."

Wow, was I ever relieved about the outcome of that!

It took months to recover from the liposuction surgery. It was a very bad experience, and I ended up with one leg slightly bigger than the other. I have many nerves that were also damaged from the surgery. My suggestion to people who ask me if they should do it is, "No, just eat healthy and exercise!"

It had been slightly more than two years since my mother's death, and I was still mourning. Could it be the guilt for not going to visit with her when she begged me to come see her? Or could it be she died of a broken heart from my living such a sinful life? At her funeral I was confronted by one of the Mennonite pastors asking me why I was crying, that if I would change my sinful ways and come back to the Lord and return to the Mennonite faith, I may see her again in Heaven. I am thinking to myself about the remark he just made to me; why, Lord, have people (including family, pastors, followers of Yours) judged me always, my entire life? I have heard from the time I was eighteen years old that I am a sinner and going to hell.

The pastor continued saying, "Stop crying, Sharon; your mom is in Heaven and free from all of the burdens that life has brought her. She is free from all her pain and troubles, but I do know she would want for you to someday be back in the arms of the Lord. Your mom wants you to be happy living your life again for the Lord. Living apart from the Lord, there will never be hope or life abundant."

Reflecting back on my mother's funeral, the service was very long, and I sobbed through most of it. With every song they sang, I would cry even harder, especially her favorite songs. I knew I had lost my dearest friend, my mother. She was gone now and forever! I knew she was in Heaven with Jesus who she lived for every day, trying to always please Him. He was on her mind always since the day she fell in love with Him when she accepted Him as her Lord and Savior at age thirteen.

Well, when I was soon to celebrate my fiftieth birthday, I was still thinking about my mother every day. I missed her more then than ever. As a child and teenager, she was always the first person whom I embraced upon finishing my school day; and when anything good happened to me, she was always there with encouraging words and smiles. My mother believed in me, and she wanted me to be happy. I didn't realize how much she really still loved me until one of my Mennonite sisters told me after the funeral service that she would pray for me every day, asking God to open my eyes and show me the way to the "good life," living for the Lord. She would say to my siblings how much she missed me and wished she could see me one more time before she passed on.

Down deep I was beginning to feel like a failure as a daughter, a mother, and a sister. I started thinking about leaving Patrick and Nicole behind with their father. Since the day I left them, I lingered through every day, thinking about them, and the hurt they must feel. Who was I becoming? How could I walk away from my precious children? I began hating myself. A thickening layer of callousness covered my heart, preventing me to having peace in my life.

Making money was my objective, the more I made the more I could spend on improving my home, my looks, and, of course, spoiling my children with awesome trips and gifts and more gifts. There was no rest for me; I wanted it all!

I wanted perfection in my life and appearance. I would shop almost every day for a new outfit. I was having electrolysis procedures done weekly to remove all the peach fuzz from my face. I was having laser treatments once a month to remove brown spots from my face due to tanning; Botox injected around my eyes and forehead to remove the fine lines. I thought being perfect was going to bring me happiness.

I was very fortunate that my work was my passion. I couldn't wait to get my day started at 5:00 a.m. I enjoyed going on appointments; I would schedule at least three appointments a day. I was in love with my job! My closure rate for closing sales on first appointments was unbelievably high; close to 90 percent. I was told by many people that I could sell ice to the Eskimos.

Again, I will always be grateful to my mother for inspiring me at a very young age to be the best person by showing kindness, being a good listener, and always giving compliments.

PART III

THE GOOD LIFE

Chapter 33

HONESTY WAY

Over thirty years of being neglected and rejected would damage anyone's heart. I found that choosing to live my life without God the last thirty years was beginning to take a toll on me due to some bad choices I had made.

Tommy and I had a house built about two years before, but our relationship was taking a plunge really fast. I knew he was not being faithful to me. I told him one day I was through with his double-standard relationship with me. The day he moved out, he said to me, "Sharon, I thought we were going to grow old together; what happened?" I knew I could not trust him; he had a wandering eye. I often invited him to go to church with me, but his response was always, "I am not interested in the church thing." We said our final goodbyes and he was gone.

One morning when I was in Florida on business, I thought to myself why not give God a chance again? I have exhausted myself from living on the wild side. Sitting on the beach, watching the sun rise above the high waters, my heart was being stirred with the thought that God wants to use me to help others that are brokenhearted, and are consumed with despair, especially my sister Ann Marie. During the week in Florida I realized I had been running away from all my problems. I wanted benevolence like my longtime church friend Jeanette. I had wanted for a long time and would often say to myself, "Someday I am going to have so much love, joy, and peace in my heart like Jeanette."

My mind, for the last five years has been a battlefield struggling with the enemy (Satan). I was trying to put my complete trust in God, but I was believing lies that I would never have a fulfilling life because of my past, committing sin after sin and that I was not a good person, not having what it takes to be a successful business person. I wanted to believe the contrary: I do matter; I am a good person. I wanted to believe that God wants to give me all of His "Great and precious promises," as in 2 Peter 1:3-4 "His divine power has given us everything we need for life and godliness through our knowledge of Him who called us by his own glory and goodness." (Through these He has given me His very great and precious promises, so that through them I may participate in the divine nature and escape the corruption in the world caused by evil desires.)

As I was reflecting back on my life, sitting on the beach, I remembered having dreams of sharing my life with a partner who had a relationship with God. I would often think of Darren. Actually, I would pray, asking God if I could possibly experience life with a godly man before my life on earth was over, but I knew in the back of my mind that it is not about finding the right person but becoming the right person. I knew I would need to do an overhaul on my way of living.

Looking toward the horizon, I saw a big vessel out in the water. The vessel looked so lonely out there, the way I felt at that moment, lost and lonely. I began praying,

> Dear Heavenly Father, I want to receive Your love and grace in my life. Please forgive me Lord for all the bad choices I have made in my life. I know it has grieved you for all the sins I have committed, especially the abortions, which to me is such a horrific

sin; I hear "a murderer" echoing in my ears constantly. Please take away my heavy burden of this and replace it with Your mercy as it says in Psalm 103:12, God promises to remove our sins "as far as the east is from the west."

Please, Lord, guide me with Your hand and show me the best life yet in store for me. I know You will take me there; I just need to put my complete trust in You. I know, dear Lord, your heart for me is love, not hate. I receive Your forgiveness for my abortions and the multitude of other sins. I know You want me to forgive myself so my life can be filled with peace and Your rest. From this day forward, I will rest in Your mercy and Your love for me.

I knew I had to let go all the anger that had been stored deep inside me for many decades. I was fifty years old, and not a day had passed by without thinking about having been bullied in middle school and high school, banned from youth meetings, cast out by the church; harrassed sexually in the workplace; and abused in my relationships. I had so many wounds, and I guessed they would be there for a lifetime, but I knew, with the Lord in my life again, I could focus on Him and His promises that He would mend my wounds since He is the best healer. I left all my pain from the past in God's hands since He is in control of how justice would be served to those who have wronged me. Living in intense animosity is not worth the trouble, while happiness is worth any price.

This was the beginning of my new life, wrapped in a new robe on the beach; asking God to help me to forgive all those who have hurt me, just as He had forgiven me for rebelling against Him. My prayer was interrupted when I heard Him speak softly to my heart (it was not an audible voice), "Sharon, I still love you," and then I felt His arms wrapped around me. It was just that spark needed to reignite my depleting faith. I was back in His arms again. I was finally free from the enemy, and I would never be bound by the enemy again. My heart soared with hope and I knew then that God had a better plan for me!

I continued praying, asking forgiveness for the hurt I had caused my parents. A sibling asked me once if I was sorry for sending our parents to the grave before their time. I realized that I had caused tremendous pain for so many of my family members.

A verse in the Bible that I often referred to as a young teenager popped into my mind as I sat looking into the deep waters (Mark 11:22-24).

> Then Jesus said to the disciples, 'Have faith in God. I tell you the truth, you can say to this mountain, 'May you be lifted up and thrown into the sea,' and it will happen. But you must really believe it will happen and have no doubt in your heart. I tell you, you can pray for anything and if you believe that you've received it, it will be yours.

Honestly, I was ready to have that faith again. I knew in my mind that mankind was not the answer to having a blessed life. We live in an imperfect world with imperfect people. God, and He alone, is the answer to everything; He will provide for those that truly believe in Him. Whether you're soaring like an eagle or falling toward rock bottom, God is there to catch you. His faithfulness will never fail.

I remember as a young child my dream was to travel the world bringing the unsaved to Jesus, and Mom would say, "Sharon, if you have God with you, and you completely trust in Him, and if it is God's will, your dream will be reached." My father had high expectations for me as a very young teenager, and he would say to me, "Sharon, I am praying that you find your value, significance, and true life's meaning in God alone. With God's blessing, He will take you wherever you want to go."

I have been in the interior design business for almost twenty years. My business is doing very well, since I have the best person working with me, God. I know I have His blessings as every day I feel his presence. It is God who has spared my life when I was living on the wild side. It will be God who will care for me financially, and it will be Him who will take care of all my needs. God is giving me another opportunity to experience life with Him again. I am ready to use the gifts, the talents, and the creative abilities He has given me to help improve the community, and hopefully make a difference in the people's lives who are wearing my old robe (my past). May my dark times teach me to help others on similar paths as I have traveled.

It has been painful and embarrassing to reflect back on my disturbing past, but I know God has forgiven me, because I have peace in my heart. My new robe fits me so much better, and I even have more room to grow with the Lord. Life is a gift from God, and I was very lucky that I had parents praying for me every day to keep me safe, that I may one day return to the God of my youth before it was too late. Their prayers were answered. I am looking forward to seeing my mom and dad in Heaven.

It says in Proverbs 22:6 "Train a child in the way he should go and when he is old, he will not depart from it." This means a child's foundational values will stick with him or her for the rest of that child's life. Today, child development experts also have agreed that the majority of a child's personality is in place at a very young age. I have found my happy spirit again, and because of my parents' perfect teachings of His Word, I have found my inspiration in Jesus again. I have not found religion, and I do not plan on returning to the Mennonite faith. I have found God Himself and His perfect love, and Jesus is my best friend again. God has my back and my hand. God has my highest praise. I am serving God in my own way, the way in which He made me. God created each of us with different interests, different personalities, different looks, different needs, and different IQs, but each of us can enjoy Him right here and now as we were made. I have invited God into my life, to lead me every moment of the day and transform my life into something awesome and beautiful.

I know in my heart and soul that I do not need to be a Mennonite to be His follower and that not being a Mennonite will not keep me out of Heaven. Actually, I was born twenty years too early. There are a few sects of Mennonites today whose women do not wear their coverings at all; they also wear slacks, jewelry, and makeup. They have TVs and participate in most worldly pleasures. A few years ago I stopped by Lancaster Mennonite High School, and not one teacher I saw was wearing a covering. The students were dressed same as the world and were not wearing coverings. The dorms were co-ed. As I was walking through the dormitories, I glanced into a room with a boy and a girl chatting and working on an assignment together.

I approached an African American male outside the dormitory as he was shooting a basketball into the hoop and asked him, "Are you a Mennonite?"

He replied, "Yes, I am!"

I asked, "Are you from Pennsylvania?"

"No, I am from California but this is the best Christian High School in the world," he said with so much enthusiasm!

Also, after thirty-plus years, I am inspired again to be a Christlike person. It's time for this generation to shed some of the burdensome trappings of denominationalism and return to the simple faith rooted in discipleship. Let's love one another and show compassion and kindness like Jesus taught his disciples when He was here on earth. Denominationalism is a spirit that keeps us bound in the traditions of men, prejudices, and pride. We must be free of them in order to progress in God's kingdom mentality. God does not want our religion/denomination, He wants a relationship with us.

I remember as a child that my parents instilled many positive qualities in me, my siblings, and the community, such as showing kindness, having peace and joy in our hearts, and showing compassion for others as Jesus taught his followers. It was instilled in me that positive qualities and thoughts bring positive results, such as caring and sharing, good health, happiness, and prosperity. My mother would often say, "Keep the negative thoughts out since they only will bring you fear, dislike, anxiety, poverty, and misery." My mom would remind the community to have faith in God and He would provide for all our needs. My parents were a blessing to so many people as I reflect back on my early childhood and young teenage years.

I am putting my faith in God that he will enrich my life by giving me all of His "great and precious promises" (2 Peter 1:4). My children did not have the same upbringing as I had, but with God in my life again, hopefully I can set an example to them of the new me. The Bible says in II Timothy 1:5 "Fan the flame of my gift in your children. Sincere faith can be passed on to your children and to their children from generation to generation. Keep passing on a heritage of faith. Don't let my flame go out." My prayer is that my children will keep the flame going.

I know God will give me guidance in showing my children that He is real and He is the Creator of this magnificent universe. I know He is real because I feel His presence always and His push to keep me going. I do believe God has His hands on us, and I know He has a plan for each one of us so we need to *believe* and have *faith* in Him. He has a reason and a purpose for why we have good and bad challenges in life.

Alan Redpath says it well:

> There is nothing—no circumstance, no trouble, no testing—that can ever touch me until, first of all, it has gone past God and past Christ, right through to me. If it has come that far, it has come with a great purpose, which I may not understand at the moment, but as I refuse to become panicky, as I lift up my eyes to him and accept it as coming from the throne of God for some great purpose of blessing to my own heart, no sorrow will ever disturb me, no trial will ever disarm me, no circumstance will cause me to fret, for I shall rest in the joy of who my Lord is.

Chapter 34

GLOWING DAYS PATHWAY

$\mathcal{I}$t's Valentine's Day, and I am shopping for a special card today for my childhood sweetheart. It's been so long since I've experienced any sort of attention or expressions of love on this day. Valentine's Day had become like most other days for many years. Almost a year ago, a spark was lit and right now it is a full-fledged, four-alarm fire that can be seen as far as the east is from the west! That's right; I am on fire for my soul mate that God has brought back into my life. My childhood beau has ignited a fire of love and passion within me that I didn't think was possible or that words can describe. He has renewed the very essence and core of my being. I'm alive. I am a new person. I have hope, joy and love again!

The past year has been so incredible for me due to rekindling my friendship with my childhood soul mate. He is a Heaven-sent gift from God. I remember praying to God, asking Him to send me a godly man to experience life with if it was His will, and He sent to me the most special and compassionate man in the whole-wide world. Today, this Valentine's Day is very special. I now have a reason to want to celebrate and share the message of love that this day is about, because of Darren, my Valentine. I have found the perfect card to give my Valentine; the card sums it up so well how I truly felt in my heart and soul, saying:

You are my everything; You are my passion that sweeps me away from the craziness of this world to that beautiful romantic place in your arms where my body and soul feel so at home.... You are the reason why I'm happier than I ever imagined I could be.... You are my heart's true love and my wildest dream come true.

We are celebrating our first Valentine's Day together ever, by having dinner at a wonderful restaurant on the water. We had so much to say and share with each other since it has been thirty-four years since we had seen each other.

Darren began, saying, "Where do I begin?"

I answered, "I've often heard the beginning is the best place to start. "

Darren was almost whispering,

Okay, my dear, in the beginning there were two child-hood friends. They grew up together. They played together. They shared each other's families. They grew from friends to lovers. It was beautiful; they laughed together; they shared their thoughts and dreams together; they shared their beliefs together; most of all they were each other's first love. Yes, you, Sharon, were my first love! The two childhood friends became boyfriend and girlfriend and lovers in their own way. They stayed that way through the end of high school years and early college days. And then it happened, whether it was distance, immaturity, or just flat out stupidity and ignorance, he let her go. He didn't do what he needed to; she wanted him to keep the relationship alive!

You know when we first started talking again about a year ago, you told me you were sorry if you hurt me when you ended our relationship. You said that you had made a mistake. The truth is, you're not to blame, I am. Maybe if I would have paid attention to what you were saying in your letters and at least written to you, come home, maybe the two childhood sweethearts might have married, but they didn't. They each went their separate ways, for better or for worse.

There is one thing I do know for certain and that I'm thankful for today is that the Lord blessed my life with two of the most precious and dearest persons in my life, my two sons. And I also know this is true for you, you've been blessed with Patrick, Nicole, and Jared. The way you talk about your children is so special and a blessing for me. You know, I've noticed a different reflection in your voice when you tell me about your children. It is neat that your daughter is your best friend—someone you can share your innermost thoughts and secrets with.

Getting back to my story, it really wasn't you alone that caused our breakup. It was me. I didn't keep my end of the commitment that I believe you wanted back then. We went our separate ways, you with Dale and me with Karen. Even though we were separated by time and distance, the first love feelings, though faint at times, still glowed. I know it did with you, and it did with me also. I was always hoping to see you or to hear how you were doing by talking to my mother. First love feelings never vanish. They may dim and get suppressed, but they are always there and alive!

I thank God every day for you and for Him allowing you to be back in my life. Sharon, you do complete me. Despite my shortcomings, you build me up, you make me feel special. You boost my confidence. You make me feel like no one has ever done before. I know you are my soul mate, and we will be together forever. I do know, without a doubt, that your prayers, your hopes, your persistence, your dream and desire for us to be back together again is an answered prayer from God!

Almost a year ago the Lord blessed my life in a way that words cannot describe. That was the first day that our reunion and union began. I'll never be able to repay you or do anything sufficient enough to let you know how much I love you or could thank you to the degree you deserve. It is because of you that we're together again. And, believe me, I'll never again make the same mistake I did almost thirty-four years ago by letting you go.

Despite the thirty-four years of being separated, we childhood friends and lovers did experience some of the same sad life stories. Our mutual love for our spouses evaporated. We each experienced many years of unhappiness, loneliness, and, at times, despair. We each knew that their lives were incomplete and restless. However, despite this, we still persisted. We found hope and strength in and through their children.

And yes, you, Sharon, despite all of the obstacles you experienced in most of your relationships with men, you survived and how you've survived! You're a self-made woman, a successful businesswoman and mother. For what you've accomplished and how you've done it, you are my inspiration! I remember that precious little blonde on Rocky Road with all of her energy and excitement, and now I'm blessed to enjoy the final product. I am the luckiest man on the face of this earth.

After many years of suffering, you left your marriage and ventured out on your own. You found, as I always believed you knew, that you were a survivor. You worked hard and played hard. You have become a very prominent and successful businesswoman. All that you want now is to complete your life quest, finding the man that God intended you to have. Well, my love, look no further; I am here for you. Yes, I know that God ultimately meant for you and me to be together as friends and hopefully someday in a committed relationship. I hope that I'm the one who can complete your story here on earth and in heaven, together, with you forever.

Sharon, you are the most beautiful woman I've ever known. Your physical beauty is unsurpassed, while your inner beauty is God's gift to those of us that you come in contact with. Your radiance is like a diamond sparkling in the sunlight, which melts me. You may think there are things you need to change, but I don't. You are God's special gift to me, and that is as awesome as it gets. I know I've asked you many times, why me?

So how does your story end? As for me, I want to be with you and have all of you for the days I have left on this earth, but your story's ending, I believe, is you being restored in your relationship with God.

"So, sweetheart, that is my story I wanted to share with you on our special celebration, Valentine's Day. Will you be my Valentine?

With tears of joy, I began, "Today I have a reason to celebrate and share the message of love that this day is about because of you. Yes, you are my Valentine! Being in your presence, talking to you even if it is on the telephone is incredible. I never imagined my life could be filled with so much happiness."

Darren added as he reached for my hand, "It will be my duty to see that you're the happiest person on this earth each and every day!"

As Darren stood up from the table, I commented how much weight he had lost.

Darren replied, "I want to look my best for you, Sharon."

I answered, "Darren you do not have to change a thing, but don't lose too much more weight or you will lose your pants."

He chuckled and said, "I don't think so."

I replied, "Look how loose your pants are!" With my hands tugging below his waistline, his pants dropped to the floor!

He stood there frozen with his pants down in the restaurant, and I started laughing so hard that tears were streaming down my face.

As Darren pulled his pants up with his tiger eyes gleaming at me, he said, "Sharon, you were the best thing that ever happened to me until now" and he laughingly said, "I enjoy laughing with you. I love your laugh, your happy spirit, and your enthusiasm about life. God has sent the most special and precious person in the whole wide world into my life, that's crazy you! It's like the song 'When God made you he must have been thinking about me'! You are the golden treasure at the end of my rainbow," Darren added.

As we were walking out, I reached for his hand, thanking him for a fabulous dinner and, smiling, said, "For in you is my hope, my joy, and love! And you are my love story! You are my beginning and ending. We started as each other's first love, and we'll finish as each other's last love. I think that is so neat; that is good stuff. This is the stuff stories are made of. I've never had anyone who makes me feel so special and alive like you do."

Darren put his arm around me as we walked to the car and whispered in my ear, "You have given me a new beginning, a new hope, a new joy, and a love that totally consumes and captivates me. You are my world of difference; you have made a difference in my world."

APPENDIX I

INSPIRATION FOR A
FULFILLING LIFE

RISE AND SHINE WAY!

Since I have made some changes to my lifestyle and having God first in my life again, not another man, I have found that loving one another, showing kindness, having a single faith, having peace and joy in my heart, and, most importantly, having happiness and sharing laughs with others can make our community a happy place for all to share. Our good to the community depends on how much we go out of our way to help others. We need to share our lives and be genuinely concerned for those who need help. We must show a real love for each other. We need to express the kind of love with real depth and have an understanding heart. The community and world is crying for our love and understanding, so sharing ourselves has a deeper meaning than just giving our wealth. This sharing requires us to meet on the level of what we are rather than what we have.

I learned a few years after my father had passed away, my ex-sister-in-law's husband Mike approached me one day and shared with me his memory of my father. I had no idea he even knew my father. He had only great things to say about my dad.

Mike smiled saying, "Adam was a great man! He would rent his equipment from us, Rentals Unlimited, from time to time. When he walked through the front door we were all eager to wait on him." Mike still smiling continued to say, "He would share with us his chocolate peanut butter balls and peanut butter fudge."

My dad not only had a sweet tooth, but he also had a sweet personality and was a giver like Mom. You don't need money to make a positive mark on people, but by sharing conversations, giving words of wisdom and hope, you can make the world a happier place. I am giving back to the community as my parents did in my childhood days. I am also making sacrifices to help my struggling sister Ann Marie to have a better life. She has been living in turmoil most of her life. Our longtime friend Jeanette is there also for Ann Marie, guiding and praying with her to not give up on life. Jeanette keeps her motivated by telling her that she is worthy to have more and that she deserves to have a better life.

Ann Marie is missing Mom and Dad greatly. She is having a very difficult time accepting her loneliness without our mom here on earth. Our father passed away a few years ago with chronic heart failure. He was also ready to go when the Lord called him home, but he really enjoyed every minute of life. I had noticed a change in Dad's disposition about life over the last few years of his life. He seemed happy and full of enthusiasm again. He was calling me, wanting to know how I was doing and wanted me to share family news with him, including Richard's family.

A few weeks before Dad passed on to Heaven, he called me to say, "I love you Sharon and I owe you a big hug! Always remember I want the best for you. I am so glad that you are attending church again. You know, Sharon, it is never too late to be anything you want to be, and it is never too late to reach for the highest star. Believe in your dreams and follow them! With God in your life again you can do anything, anything!"

I thanked Dad for his inspiration and I told him that his perfect teachings of God's Word had never left me. I also told him that I loved him very much and thanked him for all his prayers. As I hung up the phone with tears trickling down my cheeks, I couldn't believe I actually heard Dad's kind words, saying he loves me and he owes me a hug; it had been over thirty years since he shared any loving words with me. There is nothing as powerful as knowing your father loves you.

About two years after Dad's death, I ran into a man who knew my dad, and he asked me, "Where is your father now?" I answered back, "He is in Heaven with my mom." He went on to say that my dad was a very kind and caring man, and he thinks about him often.

He was one of the children from the community who my dad picked up in his Sunday school bus. For many years my parents served the community well and left a positive mark on many people from my childhood/teenage era, but it all changed when I was denied communion, which was one of the reasons they left Gaithersburg Mennonite Mission Church. They became isolated from the community and the extended family unit.

Ann Marie was dealt a very bad hand in life. Her life has always been a struggle, and now without our mother and father, I need to be there for her, just as she needed me when we were young. After I accepted Jesus as my Savior and Lord when I was eleven, I brought Ann Marie to Jesus upon returning from camp. She was thirteen years old. I have reminded her again, after forty years, that she has Jesus with her, and as long as she has Jesus in her heart, God will bless her and keep her strong.

When I think of Jesus, I want to rise and shine! He is my inspiration!

His light shines in my life now and His presence is in my heart guiding me to make the right choices for a beautiful and fulfilling life. When we receive Christ as Lord and Savior, God begins a renovation process in our personalities to make us better people.

Life is about choices. In the hands of every individual is the power for good or evil. Your will, will be done. Everything you do or don't do does matter! We should constantly live with passion by radiating happiness, sweetness, and joy. There are people whose presence seems to radiate sunshine wherever they go. We want to be the people who radiate warmth and are helpful to our community. We want to be like a gulf stream, following our own course, flowing calmly and undisturbed in the ocean of cold water. We want our presence to bring a glow of sunshine to all.

There are people who float down the stream of life like icebergs: cold, reserved, unapproachable, and self-content. These people have a depressing influence on all who fall under the spell of their coldness. We have duties to others, as well as duties to ourselves. We need to give the best of ourselves. In our own personal lives, we should strive to make others happy. In doing so, we will bring much happiness into our own lives. Happiness consists not of having but of being, not of possessing but of enjoying. We are the creator of our own happiness.

As a child and up until I left my Mennonite faith I had a desire in my heart to embrace everyone with God's love for them! I had a dream that everyone in the universe would have God's love in their heart. My heart's desire was always to have Jesus formed in me, my inner being, so I could reflect His beauty in the world by doing Christ-like deeds.

My mother often reminded me that it is never too late to pursue my childhood dream. When Mom passed, I knew I had lost my dearest friend. I knew in my heart that she loved me so, so much. There is nothing like a mother's love. I felt as though my world had ended; I felt so much guilt that I never did see her before she passed. If only I could see her one more time, I would tell her how much I really did love her and her waiting is over that I am back in God's arms again.

God had used the death of my mom to bring me to total brokenness. The ever-present guilt and sorrow for the hurt I brought to my mother and father must continually be turned over to God. I had lost many years without my parents and God in my life. As mentioned in Philippians 4:6-13 and James 1:5, "Years lost are never truly regained, but God's mercy, strength and wisdom are with me in abundance for the asking."

Sometimes we have to be totally broken before God can mend us. My mother had begged me to come see her about four months before she passed. In our last telephone conversation, she mentioned she was not feeling well and had a vision in a dream that she saw Heaven and the Lord was calling her home. She added that she was ready to meet her Heavenly Father. It had been four years since I had seen her, and I promised I would visit soon, but I was really busy with my interior design business. Actually, I was ashamed of the lifestyle I was living and did not feel comfortable visiting with her. At my last visit with my parents, Dad reminded me that I was living a very sinful life, and was going straight to hell if I didn't make some changes and give God a chance again.

My last phone conversation with Mom before her death has stuck with me, "Sharon, give God a chance again, and it is never too late to pursue your childhood dream. He and your mom miss you." My mother left me a legacy—her faith in God, her love and kindness for all humanity. I only hope and pray that I can leave the same legacy with my loved ones. My mother took every opportunity to talk about God; she was a godly mother—she loved the Lord her God with all her heart, soul, mind, and strength. She passionately and consistently taught her offspring to do the same. No one has more potential for a godly influence on a child than that child's God-fearing mother.

Finding Hope

Keep hoping for the best in your life and never lose your faith in God. The instructions you follow will determine the future you create. We must unite and work for the good of mankind everywhere. We must look with hope even if at times the future is dim. We must keep our hope alive. We must fall back into the eternal arms of faith and be wise enough to say, "I will trust God" and not let little problems turn our lives in doubt.

One must have faith in oneself as a necessary ingredient to reach any degree of success in life. One must have faith in God. You cannot trust a God that you hold in your mind to be nonexistent or untrustworthy. In order to trust God or have communion with Him, one must believe He exists. Faith is the main spring of energy. It provides the zest, the push, the initiative, and the courage that is necessary to have a fulfilling life. There were times in my life when I got discouraged or became very restless about life, due to being cast out by the church and family and being bullied or unappreciated, but knowing that I had family praying for me and believing that God really never deserted me, kept me motivated to not give up, and I kept pushing toward my dreams.

Today, we find too many young adults not willing to reach for the sky. They avoid risks and shun responsibility. They wish to do well I am sure, but just enough to get by. "Wow," they comment, "I put my forty hours in this week." You must stand for more than a point of survival if you want to be successful and help make this world a better place in the future. We need to be fruitful by using the gifts that were given us at birth and keep reaching for the stars.

We need to *rise and shine* because there is so much darkness covering our universe. What are we doing about the young? We need to empower our children to reach their full potential. Are we setting a good example for them to become respectful young adults? What are we doing about improving the quality of life for the future? We need to get our young people motivated to be Christ-like. The world is tugging at our children's hearts, pulling them down and away from God. We need to really love our children. Loving our children means we are willing to get down in the trenches and fight to turn our children's hearts toward God.

We need to teach our children the spiritual significance of marriage, keeping God centered in their marriage.

We need to speak out on having *world peace, no more wars*!

Do not judge others! Life is as personal as death itself, with every man being responsible only to himself and Almighty God for his actions. Again, I stress to you: let God do the judging. Your religion need not be my religion. Your pleasures need not be my pleasures. Your fears need not be my fears. Compassion is the key; have unconditional love and do not judge others. Judgment is bondage whether we're judging ourselves or others.

My prayer today and every day is, "Please dear God may I love others in the same spirit in which you love them, unconditionally and full of grace." Let's love one another! If you do not have love, you have nothing. You need to start by loving yourself before you can love anyone else. What is love? First Corinthians 13 defines love. It says,

"Love is patient; love is kind and envies no one. Love is never boastful, nor conceited, nor rude; never selfish, not quick to take offense. Love keeps no score of wrongs; does not gloat over men's sins, but delights in the truth. There is nothing love cannot face; there is no limit to its faith, its hope, and its endurance.

Love is the key to happiness. It teaches us humility, understanding and self-respect. Love, like commitment, involvement, and concern, must be put into action. Always try to have enough love to share with your friends; pour it on your children and teach them that the secret to life is *love*. Try to be down to earth yet have sufficient wisdom to reach for the highest star. Always try to look at life with a cheerful and loving heart.

We need to *rise and shine,* and with living our life, we need to keep God in our heart.. God is loving and so forgiving. He gave us a gift at birth and while in our mother's womb, He had our destiny planned for us. His plan for us is intended to bless us and give us a future and hope. God is ready to give you all His great and precious promises. Reach for the stars because if you have God with you, there is nothing or nobody that is going to stand in your way!

A person who is unselfish, kind, loving, tender, helpful, ready to lighten the burden of those around him, to hearten the struggling one, and to forget himself sometimes in remembering others is on the right road to a full and complete life. Enjoy the "good life" by making the right choices and letting go of all your fears. We have only one light and one life so make the best of it! So rise and let your light shine; *don't hide it under a bushel! No!*

It was Nelson Mandela who sums it up well on how to make a world of difference in your life and others by letting go of your fears. Do not live in fear. God can overcome our fears no matter what they are.

"The face of fear can be very scary, but once you allow yourself to feel your fear and step beyond it, to the other side, it is absolutely beautiful on the other side. For on the other side of fear ... love, freedom, fulfillment is patiently waiting. I cannot profess that

I will always bring this to my mind, but I try to remember that my fear has a very bright side. Go ahead, feel your fear, but give it a hug, as you would any good friend, then step beyond it, and experience the huge sense of love, freedom and fulfillment on the other side. On the other side of your fear, you will find your Greatness, your Truth, your Love for yourself, your Self Expression, your Passions, your Integrity, the abundance, the possibilities and the life you always wanted. They were always there … you just couldn't see them through your fear. It is our deepest light, not our darkness, that most frightens us. We ask ourselves, "Who am I to be brilliant, gorgeous, talented and fabulous?" Actually, who are you not to be? You are a child of God. Your playing small doesn't serve the world. There is nothing enlightened about shrinking so that other people won't feel secure around you. We were born to make manifest the Glory of God that is within us. It's not just in some of us. It's in everyone and, as we let our light shine, we unconsciously give other people permission to do the same. As we are liberated from our own fear, our presence, automatically liberates others."

The world needs a miracle! *Be a part of the miracle* by sharing your kindness, knowledge, and God's love! Be a world changer!

Celebrate Your Life Moments

Life is a *journey* of happiness and sorrow,
Of yesterday's memories and hopes for tomorrow,
Of *pathways* we choose and detours we face
With patience and laughter, courage and grace,
Of love that we've shared and of people we've met,
Who have touched us in ways we will always remember.

INSTRUCTIONS FOR A GOOD LIFE (VOICE OF THE WISE)

I have asked many of my friends, clients, and family to share words of wisdom to having a fulfilling life. Mom would have turned seventy on her next birthday so in her honor I want to share the following seventy extensive knowledge thoughts.

1. "No Bullying" should be one of the Ten Commandments.
2. Make an impact on your community.
3. Show kindness and love to all.
4. Doing good deeds will improve your life.
5. Live everyday to the fullest with joy.
6. Happiness keeps you sweet and successful.
7. Difficulties make you stronger.
8. Show enthusiasm in everything you do.
9. Gossip is the same as murder; it kills reputations.
10. Choose your friends wisely.
11. Remember God is a loving and forgiving God.
12. Choosing happiness is the way to live your life.
13. Encourage your children to always do their best and be the best!
14. Share laughs and tell a joke.
15. Having God in your life will bring you peace, joy, and happiness.
16. Never let anyone mistreat you.

17. Cultivate relationships that enrich your life, mission, and goals.
18. Focus on solutions, not problems.
19. Mistakes make you humble.
20. Success makes you shine.
21. Only true friends make you feel comfortable and free.
22. Never laugh at or discourage anyone's dreams.
23. Don't judge people by their relatives.
24. Overcome thought patterns that hinder success.
25. Call your mother and grandmother.
26. When you lose, don't lose a lesson.
27. Remember the 3R's: Respect for self, Respect for others, and Responsibility for all your actions.
28. Smile when picking up the phone. The caller will hear it in your voice.
29. Spend some time alone.
30. Open your arms to change, but don't let go of your values.
31. Read more books and watch less TV.
32. Live a good and honorable life so when you get older and think back, you will get to enjoy it a second time.
33. A loving atmosphere in your home is so important. Do all you can to create a tranquil and a harmonious home.
34. Tell your children how much you love them.
35. Hug your child and don't forget to give them a kiss.
36. If you want your dreams to come true, you must not oversleep.
37. Of all the things you wear, your expression is the most important.
38. The best vitamin for making friends is B1.
39. The happiness of your life depends on the quality of your thoughts.
40. The heaviest thing you can carry is a grudge.
41. Ideas won't work unless "you" do.
42. Your mind is like a parachute—it functions only when open.
43. Share your knowledge. It is a way to achieve immortality.
44. Pray. There is immeasurable power in it.

45. If you make a lot of money, put it to use helping others while you are living. That is wealth's greatest satisfaction.
46. Remember that your character is your destiny.
47. The best relationship is one where your love for each other is greater than your need for each other.
48. Be gentle with the earth.
49. Mind your own business; do not judge.
50. Once a year go someplace where you have never been before.
51. Life is not about finding ourselves but about creating ourselves.
52. Worry is a sin; it only makes you feel miserable so have faith in God!
53. You can become quite remarkable when you believe in yourself.
54. People see you the way you see yourself, so always be your best!
55. Positive thinking is the way to think!
56. Read a good book.
57. Join a church.
58. You are too valuable to have the wrong people in your life.
59. See yourself as an altogether new person; one who is excited, vital, and vigorous.
60. Start every day by affirming peaceful and happy attitudes.
61. Say nice and encouraging words to the people in your life.
62. Pour your love and wisdom on your children.
63. Learn a song and sing it.
64. Make the right choices!
65. Eat ice cream!
66. Start your day reading your Bible.
67. Wake up looking on the bright side!
68. Make someone happy!
69. Learn to enjoy the simple things in life!
70. The Ten Commandments are not multiple choice.

If you follow the above instructions and keep God in your life, you will have a very fulfilling and blessed life. Looking back on my life, I have evidence (my story) that everything you do and don't do matters for a life time! Be your *best* always!

Start Working on Your Legacy!

Cheers to your best life ever! Make a positive mark on someone and it will be remembered for a lifetime. Also, leave your mark in the world by leaving behind children who grow up to love and serve the Lord and who then also raises godly children to continue your godly legacy for generations to come.

CPSIA information can be obtained at www.ICGtesting.com
Printed in the USA
BVOW03s1408171114

375459BV00003B/5/P